WEBSTER'S
Challenging
Large Print
Crossword
Puzzles

Selected by the Editors of Merriam-Webster

**FEDERAL
STREET
PRESS**

A Division of Merriam-Webster, Incorporated
Springfield, Massachusetts

This edition published by Federal Street Press, a Division of Merriam-Webster, Incorporated
P.O. Box 281
Springfield, MA 01102

Federal Street Press books are available for bulk purchase for sales promotion and premium use.
For details write the manager of special sales, Federal Street Press, P.O. Box 281, Springfield, MA 01102

ISBN 10 ISBN 1-892859-93-9
ISBN 13 ISBN 978-1892859-938

Printed in Canada
05 06 07 08 09   5 4 3 2 1

FRUIT BASKET

by Matt Gaffney

ACROSS

1. With 31-Down, Silhouettes hit
5. Sward
8. Winter warmer-upper
14. "Family Ties" role
15. Gilbert & Sullivan princess
16. Jeans measurement
17. Hole in the ground
20. Desert killer
21. Nimbi
22. Set dressings
23. Less than: prefix
24. Watch covertly
26. Asian people
27. "There oughta be —!"
31. Ohio valley planter
39. Former RSA province
40. Latin American hot spots
41. Aesir member
42. "Losing My Religion" band
43. Org. of Pippen
46. George's epithet
47. "Hill Street Blues" actor
52. Lit
54. Fauna collection
57. Youthful entrepreneurs, often
60. Dickens lad
61. Neither's mate
62. Haifa's carrier
63. Piano parts
64. Boob tubes
65. Pedro's paw

DOWN

1. Big do
2. Students at 25-Down
3. Holiday helper
4. Notch maker
5. Abs firmer
6. Pervasive atmosphere
7. Andrews and Delany
8. Peg game
9. "Movin' —" ("The Jeffersons" theme)
10. Sovereign of old
11. Actor Ikonen
12. Noted lawman
13. Irving and Lowell
18. In denial?
19. Clairvoyance
23. Author Arendt
25. CT school
26. Waldheim's predecessor
28. Man with a renowned band

Crossword grid with numbered cells: 1, 2, 3, 4, 5, 6, 7, 8, 9, 10, 11, 12, 13 (row 1); 14, 15, 16 (row 2); 17, 18, 19 (row 3); 20, 21, 22 (row 4); 23, 24, 25 (row 5); 26, 27, 28, 29, 30 (row 6); 31, 32, 33, 34, 35, 36, 37, 38 (row 7); 39 (row 8); 40 (row 9); 41, 42 (row 10); 43, 44, 45, 46 (row 11); 47, 48, 49, 50, 51, 52, 53, 54, 55, 56 (row 12); 57, 58, 59 (row 13); 60, 61, 62 (row 14); 63, 64, 65 (row 15)

Solution is on page 214

29. Rocker Rick

30. "— to please"

31. See 1-Across

32. Mouths

33. Be pining

34. Lib. location

35. Earlier beginning?

36. Vim

37. Series ender

38. Plaines preceder

44. Nasty

45. 10%-er

46. Losers in 1902

47. Pig repast

48. Soccer great

49. Surrounded by

50. Variable star

51. Scott Turow book

53. Ukraine town

54. *Nana* author

55. Algerian port

56. Skagerrak port

58. It's *longa*

59. Rep.'s foe

3

2 ROCKY REPORT

by David King

ACROSS

1. Sound of a sabot
5. Famous freebooter
9. Mandibles
14. Oater writer Grey
15. Stocking shade
16. Talk-show icon
17. Singer James
18. Rely (on)
19. Spine-tingling
20. Rocky's cookie additives
23. Like, cool
24. Bad spell
25. Bad spell
26. Blue bird that talks a blue streak
27. Arizona city
28. Where losers go?
31. *Brand* playwright
34. Wizard
35. Give tit for tat
36. Fails to appreciate Rocky?
39. Shell holder
40. A Gibb
41. Swatch competitor
42. Equivocate
43. Pet name for a pet
44. Casual dance
45. Nobelist Morrison
46. Fix
47. Bat material
50. Rocky's parting words?
54. Go lance to lance
55. Winter ditty
56. Splendor
57. One of the haves
58. Mythic meanie
59. Shawm's kin
60. Ms. Friedan
61. Optimistic
62. Spree

DOWN

1. Pizen native
2. Wood turner
3. Drafty?
4. Set of chimes
5. Nimoy costar
6. Mountaineering tool
7. "Phooey!"
8. Surfer's wheels
9. Canaan conqueror
10. Bibliographer's abbr.
11. Shawl, e.g.
12. Late husband, on "Phyllis"
13. Circumspect
21. Asian inns
22. Person with promise

4

Solution is on page 214

26. WWII vehicle

27. Watered sites

28. Not sink

29. Cracker spread

30. Peak point

31. Skin woe

32. Loft item

33. Take from the take

34. Church title

35. Use shears

37. Regional animals

38. Puny bits

43. Frost's forte

44. *Airport* author

45. Remote target?

46. Crowd taunts

47. Unbaked brick

48. Pacific islands

49. All nerves

50. Inventor Elias

51. Cousin's mom

52. NASA stopper

53. Fleck

54. Headhunter's bait

by Gus Black

ACROSS

1. CLXX x X
5. Crack from exposure
9. Parish cleric
14. Wife of Jacob
15. Keep on the move
16. Philanthropist's claim
17. Significant events?
20. Piper who picked
21. Easter event
22. Really wretched
25. Palmer or Perry
26. Sea of Azov feeder
27. Atomic item
28. Nice region
29. Myrmecophile's housemate
30. *Tootsie*'s Garr
31. Flemish artist
33. Muffin-pan pastry?
38. Fife player
39. Sites for scientists
41. Canine command
44. People on the other side
45. Ogle
47. In the manner of
48. Lowly COs
49. European republic
50. — Mae (student loan funding)
52. Hammered instruments
53. Wasteful in major matters?
58. Cain's boy
59. Admiral qualifier
60. Germ cell
61. End of the line
62. Concerning
63. Proofreader's prey

DOWN

1. Civil-rights monogram
2. Agnus —
3. 1984 film about Northern Ireland
4. Eating tool
5. Modern Minoan
6. Urban inn
7. Prove true
8. According to
9. Ascorbic acid
10. Composer Stravinsky
11. Trudeau's land
12. Photographer Richard
13. Take umbrage at
18. Office note
19. Muffet's bane
22. Fitting

Solution is on page 214

23. Engendered

24. Long ago

25. Is in accord

28. Mongrels

31. Ceremonies

32. King thriller

34. Airborne

35. Riot profiteer

36. River between Europe and Asia

37. Abba of Israel

40. Porcine pen

41. Sunned

42. Galahad's mom

43. Run all-out

45. Maiden in "The Raven"

46. Hence

49. Make it big

51. Bats

52. Hoover's horde

54. Uris hero

55. Wall climber

56. Eat late

57. Medical-care meddler, to some

by M.D. Randolph

ACROSS

1. Auto emission
6. Indonesian island
10. Aswan's waterway
14. Divided
15. Mangle alternative
16. Tiki, for example
17. Butt out?
20. Target
21. Cask dregs
22. Coquette
23. Egg container
24. Playbill roster
26. Altitude measurer
29. Sauntered
32. Pi followers
33. Cliffhanger element
34. FDR program
36. Vent?
40. Verily
41. Garment feature
42. Ploy
43. Sun circlers
45. Disraeli portrayer
47. — majesty
48. Heed
49. In the first place
52. Summers, in Pau
53. Conservationist gp.
56. Antithesis of "Absence makes the heart grow fonder"?
60. Rainer role
61. Oracular opening
62. Preminger film
63. Grasped
64. Young salmon
65. More desiccated

DOWN

1. Bonnie player
2. Astride
3. Tennyson poem
4. Misplay
5. Hot
6. I.Q. pioneer
7. Some Wall Streeters, briefly
8. Musical Reed
9. Election winners
10. Nonagenarian's age
11. Hypothesis
12. Fast result?
13. Otherwise
18. Occident
19. *Soi*
23. Houston org.
24. French landscapist
25. Like
26. Roman revel
27. Canary call
28. Utter

Solution is on page 214

29. Ancient Iranis

30. Jadedness

31. Guise

33. Beat soundly

35. Enzyme endings

37. Scrimmage lead-in

38. Wallet fillers

39. Paris airport

44. Rose's cousin

45. Help heavies

46. Vended used

48. Different

49. Piglet's pal

50. Criterion

51. Romance lang.

52. Elbe feeder

53. Needle case

54. Wee opening

55. Remote

57. Test the Tokay

58. *Love ___ Ball* (1963 flick)

59. Nasser's realm: abbr.

COMPRESSED GAS

by Arthur S. Verdesca

ACROSS

1. Four roods
5. Post on deck
9. *Ese*
13. Paris' home
14. Above a whisper
16. Less than all
17. Bear on the person
18. Mechanism lead-in
19. English public school
20. Imported TV series
23. She in sheep's clothing
24. Dawn goddess
25. Welcome change
33. High-seas spoils
34. Parcel out
35. Corp. VIP
36. Oriental nursemaid
37. Exonerate
38. Munich missus
39. Tummy muscles
40. Certain machetes
41. Warning signal
42. Eschews formality completely
45. List ender: abbr.
46. US labor group
47. Desolate burial site
55. — the kill
56. From John Paul
57. Late Verdi opus
58. Sora, for example
59. Dog the footsteps of
60. Turns right
61. Stuart queen
62. Start of a Shakespearean title
63. Once, once

DOWN

1. Near Islands isle
2. Cut off short
3. Degenerates
4. Upper canines
5. Stumpy hound
6. "— Three Lives"
7. Corrida creature
8. Alphabet quartet
9. African fly
10. Empty talk
11. 8th-century prophet
12. Two cubed, plus two
15. Doomed
21. Plane route
22. Put in order

Solution is on page 215

25. Frozen dessert

26. Lambaste

27. Town on the Saale

28. Bread spreads

29. Camera attachment

30. Guard in the pen

31. Writer Lafcadio

32. Demustify

33. Phoenician deity

37. Notion

38. Room area

40. Not just one

41. Fat: prefix

43. Alight

44. O_2 receptors

47. — even keel

48. Town near Nazareth

49. Yuri's love

50. Milky stone

51. Catch

52. More unreal

53. March date

54. Bridge seat

55. A Gershwin

by Matt Gaffney

ACROSS

1. London sights
10. Bodily humors
15. Sergei Bubka's event
16. Handy
17. Philip II's son
18. Mediterranean sailer
19. Light metal
20. Ultimatum ender
21. Ending, of sorts
22. Embarrassed
23. Normally: abbr.
24. Give guns to
26. Fled on foot
27. Put up
29. Fabricate
31. TV adjustment
32. More mysterious
34. Room header
35. D.C. ring-toss items
36. '60s rocketry revolution
39. Data-storage item
42. Garfield, e.g.
43. Reminder
47. Enthusiastic about
48. Door part
50. First name in Japanese film
51. Simile words
52. Pisa direction
53. Batterer
55. Final authority
56. Had some changes made
58. Confidential?
60. Michaels' show, for short
61. Sweet spread
62. Truth or Consequences' locale
65. Practice piece
66. *The Accidental Tourist* author
67. Aegean isle
68. Juice makers

DOWN

1. Cornered
2. *L'Avare* playwright
3. Wedding gift
4. Curly-coated feline
5. A Gabor
6. Alley sights
7. A Bourne creator?
8. Tavern tipples
9. Runner in the buff
10. Zaftig
11. Liz Smith tidbit
12. Nation formed on July 26, 1847
13. Posh
14. Trig. functions

Solution is on page 215

23. Coll. across the river from Ciudad Juárez

25. News summary

28. Kid of oaters

30. Ratio words

31. Give — to (approve)

33. Display frames

37. Tex-Mex bars

38. Study hard

39. Nin tomes

40. Class for bugs?

41. Bowl venue

44. Silo contents

45. Spirited walker

46. Deems and Liz

49. RI campus

52. Gets around

54. Actress Anouk

57. Chinese prefix

59. Old LA radio station handle

63. Nice season

64. Letter trio

by Eric Albert

ACROSS

1. Squabble
5. Jabs
10. Songwriter Phil
14. List ender
15. For the birds
16. Words for the unwary
17. Italian entree?
20. Stone picture
21. *42nd Street* star
22. Took the hook
23. Where the gulls are
24. Market places
28. Implement
29. Blake of ragtime
30. Isle east of Java
31. Loose
35. Playwright who won two Pulitzers?
38. Sharp shout
39. Be bothered by
40. Olympian Stojko
41. Diminutive
42. Regain consciousness
43. Cook on "Bonanza"
47. Bird's instrument
48. Maid from Astolat
49. Sophocles heroine
54. Spat aftermath?
56. Author Hunter
57. Resort isle
58. Indy 500 winner Luyendyk
59. Stream plugs
60. Hoofer Buddy
61. Beret holder

DOWN

1. Printing on the page
2. Constant craving
3. Sham
4. Skipped town
5. Provincial dialect
6. In the open
7. Young foxes
8. Anvil location
9. Medicine-show nostrum
10. Radiates
11. Spicy seasoning
12. Used a whetstone
13. Hobbit's home
18. Duke and earl
19. Great passion
23. Sound
24. Promoting prurience
25. Get set to play

Solution is on page 215

26. Second son

27. Speech flaw

28. Leonine in hue

30. ___ and Nothingness

31. Thin skin

32. Babble on

33. Give out

34. Padua pronoun

36. Cardinal's title

37. 19th-century pope

41. A Turner

42. Birch drooper

43. Put a spell on

44. Slugger Tony

45. Old airline

46. Inks

47. Entanglement

49. Rock props

50. Dipterous fly

51. Child's dream disturber

52. Nice night

53. Thin sword

55. Flatfish

by Eric Albert

ACROSS

1. Rushes headlong

8. Plank producer

15. Deserved reward

16. She learns on the job

17. Fishy

18. Ballet in the blue

19. Ascribed

20. Perfect deal

21. Fancy paper

22. Mountain pass

24. "I cannot tell —"

25. Palindromic Holy Roman ruler

26. Teen wheels

28. Locks up

29. Casual coverup

31. Reddish brown

33. Compilation of reprints

35. The Love Bug

39. Civil War site

44. More than

45. Rig a deck

47. Gasp out

48. Nothing more than

49. Certain lodge member

50. *The Egg* —

51. Expand in girth

54. Lacking frills

57. News service

58. Enjoying a palaver

59. Art lover

60. Firm to the bite

61. Soaked, as tea leaves

62. Smaller and rounder

DOWN

1. God, in a 1945 movie title

2. Living

3. Pause that refreshes

4. Old Spanish coins

5. Prune print

6. Old Norse poem

7. Crop beginner

8. Basic need

9. What a diva delivers

10. Imperfection; defect

11. Accidents

12. Fills the lungs

13. Like a big cat

Solution is on page 215

14. Most licentious

23. Best

26. Park performers

27. Well oiled

30. — polloi

32. Dos Passos trilogy

34. Betray

35. Chaps, in westerns

36. Dead Sea's opposite

37. Detour

38. Inspire

40. Inspired

41. Great Duvall role

42. Sort of slow

43. Wasp weapon

46. Showed stress

52. Dark and rich

53. Art Deco illustrator

55. Go white

56. Pierce player

9 ROW/ROW/ROW

by Martin Ashwood-Smith

ACROSS

1. Fascist dictator
16. Gershwin subject
17. Tree wrappings
18. Offensive holiday?
19. Dumbo's wing
20. Supplement (with "out")
21. Recent beginning?
22. Hot time in Nimes
23. Yoko and family
25. Nones follower
27. Clergyman's title: abbr.
29. Beget
31. Dish-dropper's cry
34. Olio
37. Fast sled
38. It's been running since 1963
42. Philosopher A.J.
43. Lunar phenomenon
44. Gelignite user
45. Through
46. Emporia
50. Lofty crater rovers: abbr.
52. Rat chasers?
55. Expletive of contempt
56. Nancy friend
58. Conductance unit
60. She raised Cain
61. Polygraph pulsation, perhaps
62. Healthy habit
66. Bush boss, once
67. Woman's summer wear

DOWN

1. Anne on film
2. Clown Kelly
3. More trim
4. Capone's nemesis
5. Help through tough times
6. Vast region
7. Gross
8. *Ocho* minus *siete*
9. See 29-Across
10. Ophidian quality
11. Went (for)
12. Chou En-——
13. Resolves
14. Ball team
15. "Life — Peculiar" (Doug Cox CD)
24. Lisbon lady
26. Rock of ages?
28. Arise

Solution is on page 216

30. Balanchine ballet

32. Drivers' org.?

33. Soissons seasoning

35. Party hat, at times

36. Burn balm

38. Happy-go-lucky

39. Potato part

40. Sheer gown

41. Was a real pain

47. Compel

48. Rupee fractions

49. Satin finishes

51. CLVIII x XIII

53. Tutorial tomes

54. States

56. Some Dadaist works

57. Blackbird

59. Town on the Oka

63. Expend

64. Vane dir.

65. Road sight

by Cathy Millhauser

ACROSS

1. Practice punches
5. Give a D, say
9. Oar fulcrum
14. Unexciting
15. Gem of a car?
16. Moth-eaten
17. Fish sauce
18. Chuckleheads; dolts
19. Over
20.
23. Sound-alike for 13-Down
24. Ate at eight
25. Feeling distaste for
27. Pickled flower bud
30. Singer Lawrence
31. Thy and my
32. Adar preceder
36. Pennate

39.
42. Undistinguished?
43. Biblical parter
44. *Henry & June* character
45. Presses
47. Lasso show
49. "Wait!"
51. Journalist Alexander
54. Leo's mo.
55.
60. Notary need
62. Flat fee
63. Flat follower?
64. Funny Fields
65. Make over
66. Big rig
67. — two
68. Incite to action
69. Made a bed

DOWN

1. Desperate attempt
2. Deficient in color
3. Grace's last word
4. Ebb
5. Bow treatment
6. Swiftly
7. Lacking in passion
8. Schiaparelli of fashion
9. Common contraction
10. Darlin'
11.
12. City in Yorkshire
13. 30-Across's partner
21. Walker's destination
22. Discombobulate
26. Hunter of books
27. Male trumpeters or mutes

Solution is on page 216

28. Surrounding atmosphere

29.

30. Pre-coll. exams

33. *From — Eternity*

34. Sizzling *saisons*

35. Auction action

37. *Femme* friend

38. Betting setting

40. Dweeb

41. — living (support oneself)

46. Epithet for Ron on film

48. Klutzy

49. Must

50. — a limb

51. Pricey

52. Indian in the majority

53. Player

56. Messes up

57. Cream cookie

58. Apple variety

59. OK town

61. Padua pronoun

11 LATIN LESSON

by Norton Rhoades

ACROSS

1. From the outset, to Ovid
6. Damage
10. Hester Prynne's stigma
14. Dug for diamonds
15. Through
16. The yoke's on them
17. Layer in the news
18. *Mens — in corpore sano*
19. Get runny
20. *Video*, translated
22. London's locale
24. *Culpa* capper
27. Eastern European
29. Shade on the beach
30. From the stars
32. Send out
34. Curved plank
35. Weblike tissue
36. Soapbox standee
38. Central, classically
42. IRS exams
43. — *dixit*
46. Roman skills
49. A Sinatra
50. Poet Matthew
52. Schnitzel, e.g.
54. Not many
56. Cobb et al.
57. Lyndon's wife, really
59. Island nation
61. Babbling brook
62. Last words?
64. Arm bones
68. Single
69. Hawaiian bird
70. Black out
71. Urges (on)
72. Printer's directive
73. Livy's limit

DOWN

1. First of a famous Latin trio
2. Trade, to *Variety*
3. Lennon spouse
4. "—, *vidi, vici*"
5. Ukraine port
6. Biblical prophet
7. Grape, to Gracchus
8. Desert resort
9. Passes over
10. Latin speaker
11. Uses energy
12. Of Apollo's birthplace
13. He came to bury Caesar
21. Builder's bend
23. Private coach
24. Gym flooring

Solution is on page 216

25. Compass point

26. Gudrun slew him

28. Truth, to Tacitus

31. Frog genus

33. *Serpico* author

36. Frigga's hubby

37. Check

39. Toned down

40. Text versions

41. Pick out

44. Foxy

45. Asner and Ames

46. Build up, as interest

47. Court decision

48. Axis POW camp

50. — Darya river

51. Rejection

53. Respites

55. Chamber combo

58. Aid in wrongs

60. Jai follower

63. Like: suffix

65. Author Anaïs

66. Blackbird

67. Latin links

12 IN-DECENCIES

by Martin Ashwood-Smith

ACROSS

1. London district
5. Word from Caesar
9. Liechtenstein sights
13. Staff symbol
14. Part of Ripley's slogan
15. Big ape
16. Start of a quotation
19. Punch line?
20. Breastbones
21. He may run for the money
23. Vilify
25. More squalid
28. Navigators Islands, today
30. Lanka lead-in
32. Vane
33. Theater zone
35. Ornament
37. Universally: prefix
38. Middle of the quotation
40. Jolts
44. Undermine
46. Bullish sign?
48. Quagga cousin
51. Anthologists: abbr.
53. Carnival dance
54. Brisk, to Bartók
56. Barbera's partner
58. "To Helen" penner
59. May of movies
61. Show number?
64. End of the quotation
68. Acoustical feedback
69. Makes tracks
70. Spoken
71. Cast off
72. Long ago time
73. First Stoic

DOWN

1. Strikebreaker
2. Podrida holder
3. Bridge worker
4. Below par
5. Scenic view
6. Early anesthetics
7. Black, to Blanche
8. Brave man
9. In the style of
10. High return, on the court
11. Ambo
12. Sound investment?
17. An usher's offer
18. Thurso turndown
22. Hockey's Bobby
24. Quote author
26. Blow it
27. Quote source
28. Sellout sign

Solution is on page 216

29. Draw a bead on
31. Burned up the track
34. Egg: prefix
36. Dresden direction
39. Dogma
41. Sculptor's frame
42. Burnish

43. Federal insurance org.
45. Tatter
47. Grant portrayer
48. Microwave
49. Goes with the beau
50. Wash extra
52. Tremble

55. Foul caller
57. Star spice
60. Buck chaser?
62. Withdraw gradually
63. Skagerrak town
65. That girl
66. Grassy square
67. From A —

13 HOW'S THAT AGAIN?

by Dana Motley

ACROSS

1. Gift of Somnus
6. Role for Greta
10. Homer's boy
14. *As You Like It* lass
15. Publisher Adolph
16. Lovelorn nymph
17. Unconcealed
18. Very, in Varennes
19. MBA course
20. Drone's dictum?
23. Ethyl suffix
24. Pile
25. Post-theater date
27. Star of *Suddenly*
31. Revue segment
32. Prong
33. Moocher's markers
35. Siouan language
38. Couch potato's credo?
41. Town on the Missouri
42. Lear crony
43. Sorbets
44. Hardy protagonist
46. Ben or Jerry
48. Late reception
50. Native of 27-Down
51. New Deal org.
52. Dieter's dirge?
59. Adviser Ann's sis
61. "Smile," for one
62. Hindu ascetic
63. Queue
64. Nanjing nurse
65. City near Minneapolis
66. Salt Lake team
67. Shed a tear
68. Music store buys

DOWN

1. Sean Connery, for one
2. Son of Jacob
3. Kind of sch.
4. Land of the little people
5. Finish
6. Stow in a cedar chest
7. It's at bat?
8. In the old days
9. Estimate
10. Mayberry denizen
11. Possible proposal response
12. Alpine riser
13. Photo solution
21. Glossy fabric
22. Whitehorse locale
26. Stigma site

Solution is on page 217

27. Rodgers and Hammerstein setting

28. Quenchless

29. Lower

30. Olds items

32. However, briefly

34. Public focus

36. Gadabout

37. Latin links

39. Stand for Seurat

40. Hood's handle

45. Waffle

47. Idle one

48. Muddle

49. Range

53. Inexact quantity

54. Give way under strain

55. Invited

56. Tom Joad, e.g.

57. Zest source

58. Historic times

60. "Owner of a Lonely Heart" band

14 APT ANAGRAMS

by Andrew Rowan

ACROSS

1. Festive
5. Emulate Ms. Melba
9. Bowl over
14. *Omnia vincit* —
15. Buck chaser?
16. Cupolas
17. Sensitivity
20. Felt compassion for
21. Palindromist's cry
22. Absorbed by
23. Indian groom
25. "But as it —, it ain't" (Carroll)
27. Paradox
32. Crayola offerings
33. Major misdeed
34. Cherish
37. Fictional finish?
38. Takes another shot at
41. Energy
42. Stands on the stage
44. Global lang.
45. Bigfoot's kin
46. Apt anagram for 27-Across
50. Mexican wildcat
51. Pas
52. Slammer
55. The first of September
57. Not dead, gamewise
61. Apt anagram for 17-Across
64. Lost a lap
65. Egress
66. Olympic event
67. Beowulf, e.g.
68. Deli breads
69. Bowsprit

DOWN

1. Huff
2. *Avare*'s pronoun
3. Golf-club incline
4. Members of the Ashcan School, e.g.
5. Pod
6. George's bro
7. Ibsen heroine
8. Medieval
9. Attach
10. PC part
11. Mass agreement?
12. Lemon peel
13. Italian pronoun
18. He's got it coming
19. From Eden to Nod
24. Redact
26. Wee drams
27. Ante, often
28. Greek drink

1 2 3 4 5 6 7 8 9 10 11 12 13
14 15 16
17 18 19
20 21 22
23 24 25 26
27 28 29 30 31
32 33 34 35 36
37 38 39 40 41
42 43 44 45
46 47 48 49
50 51
52 53 54 55 56 57 58 59 60
61 62 63
64 65 66
67 68 69

Solution is on page 217

29. "I — Man" (Eurythmics song)
30. *The Woman* — (Wilder film)
31. Bond player
35. Pasta choice
36. Vent
38. Suggestive
39. London law societies
40. Conceited chaps
43. Like a good freezer
45. Joyous cries
47. Metal holders
48. Meaty strip
49. Cloth shelter
52. Painter Miro
53. Big do
54. Ripley words
56. Erotic
58. Finnic fellow
59. πr^2
60. Belgian river
62. Born
63. Reno randomizer

15 CRIMES OF FASHION

by Paul Matwychuk

ACROSS

1. End of the yr.
4. Xanthippe
7. Mercator product
10. Damp, in Dundee
13. "One Day —"
15. Do away with
17. Probable source of the mermaid legend
18. Keyboard instrument
19. With 50-Across, what a makeover artist does?
21. Not *triste*
23. Concert halls
24. Passé do
25. Fess (up)
26. Pele's org.
30. Köln conjunction
31. Where designers learn their trade?
37. Actress Best
38. Nosh in a 3-Down
39. Having a narrow fashion focus?
44. Comedian Philips
46. Socialist Luxemburg
47. "Yo!"
48. Cartoonist Walker
50. See 19-Across
54. Small strummer
55. Posing for *Vogue*?
60. Vowel neglect
61. German region
64. Sang
65. First
66. Haggard opus
67. April killjoys, for short
68. Touch: prefix
69. Pt. of HRE

DOWN

1. Lake maker?
2. Attic vowel
3. Tequila dispenser
4. Explosive
5. Correct
6. Foolish ones
7. SST speed
8. — in one's bonnet
9. Sport for the smart set
10. Desirous
11. Back on board
12. You can spare it
14. Cross shape
16. "I — Song Go..."
20. Shades on the sands
21. Revelation name
22. Belt holer
27. It follows John

Solution is on page 217

28. Feign
29. Spots
32. Clarified honey
33. Whiff
34. Biblical preposition
35. Bowl chants
36. Wall ending
39. See 4-Down

40. Apiece
41. Coarse carpet
42. Comic squeal
43. Anil, e.g.
44. Ants
45. Lettuce
49. Assay
51. Cloister garb

52. Donald's ex
53. Town-related
56. Caron flick
57. Afrikaner
58. Winds up
59. Mudder's fodder
62. Etheridge's "Yes —"
63. High peak

16 ONE BAD APPLE

by Martin Ashwood-Smith

ACROSS

1. A Jackson
6. Ordered, old style
10. Mark with — (vote)
13. Hersey setting
14. Went wetly
15. Arch
16. Verse start from Gilbert and Sullivan's *Princess Ida*
18. Semi accessories
19. Verse, Part 2
20. Chard
21. Wkr. who displays briefs
22. Sings loudly
24. Thin
27. Snap
29. *Dunciad* poet
30. Tools for vegetarians
34. Hi-fi buy
35. Verse, Part 3
36. One in a suit
37. Road posting
42. Photo finisher
43. Nobody in particular
44. Pipes up
46. Messiah
48. Porch, for Plato
49. Input (data)
50. Verse, Part 4
55. Hither's companion
56. End of the verse
58. Numerical prefix
59. What Lizzie Borden took
60. Author Ira
61. Cheese hole
62. An NCO
63. Lovely locations

DOWN

1. Gridlock
2. Garden party?
3. Barrie's barker
4. Trap
5. "Cheers" cheers
6. Rummy dessert
7. Island east of Attu
8. Cut
9. Hall-of-Famer Roush
10. Step on it
11. Explosive guy
12. Relatives of 48-Across
14. Showing sinews
17. Torquay taxes
20. He's a real clown
23. Whistle blower
24. Locales for losers
25. Ostentation

Solution is on page 217

26. Date with the judge

27. Scapegoat's burden

28. Rajput royal

31. Infamous Idi

32. Chrysler creation

33. Squash divisions

38. Okla. town

39. Bad: prefix

40. Salves

41. In unison, in a libretto

42. Got the ball rolling

45. Mess up a mop

46. Bonnie's beau

47. Bunk

48. Ditto

51. Metal scoria

52. Counter call

53. Gutter site

54. Tattooist's canvas

56. Ted played him

57. Annie double?

by Eric Albert

ACROSS

1. Bound bundle
5. Seasonal songs
10. Founding father?
14. Continual change
15. 1977 AL MVP
16. Anderson on "Easy Street"
17. Crazy vehicle?
19. Rot
20. Law professor Hill
21. Lose traction
22. *The African Queen* scriptwriter
23. Feeling of watching paint dry
25. Have class
27. Rough and rugged
30. Sub seeker's system
33. Pony player's parlor: abbr.
36. Yawning
37. Pine's kin
38. River between continents
40. Patterny painting
42. Lab burner
43. Musical key
45. Common fund
47. Cal. page
48. "Gross!"
49. Puzo subject
51. Rocker Richards
53. Done ASAP
57. Goes out
59. Wonder-full
62. 1929 event
63. Exactly
64. Crazy island?
66. Gale's dog
67. Hold dear
68. Eclipse effect
69. Cold War reg.
70. Make hard
71. Mummy's home

DOWN

1. C sharp or you'll —
2. Without equal
3. Rational
4. Strangely beautiful
5. Top kick, e.g.
6. Track treats
7. Composer Satie
8. Malapropos mirth
9. Native of Norrköping
10. Food fish
11. Crazy snack?
12. Lady of Cleves
13. Karaoke accessory
18. A Tierney
24. College concentration

Solution is on page 218

26. Egyptian serpent

28. Hiatus

29. Data diagram

31. Teen's trial

32. Use a scythe

33. Give the nod to

34. Inoffensive

35. Crazy criticism?

37. Crush underfoot

39. Forebear

41. Reddish deer

44. "— believe in yesterday"

46. Poet Garcia —

49. Foil

50. Beet dish

52. Packs firmly

54. Hong Kong neighbor

55. Sacred song

56. Pulse

57. *"— Brute?"*

58. Critical cries

60. Singer Adams

61. Stupefy

65. Solidify

by Andrew Rowan

ACROSS

1. Portal post
5. Ukase issuers of yore
10. Singles in suits?
14. Turgenev's birthplace
15. Where to find Leland McKenzie
16. Undone?
17. Nobel-winning cleric
18. Like a solipsist
20. Low life?
22. Four-o'clock feedings
23. Intellect: Latin
25. For whom the bell tolls
26. Diego's doublet
27. The gloomy dean of St. Paul's
30. Article for Alamos
33. One of Samuel Johnson's circle
38. Scandalous queen of France
39. Sot's trouble
40. Scottish river
41. Dele deleter
42. MS emenders
43. Diner order
46. Pipsqueak's problem
48. Metrical foot, in Greek verse
52. Change magazines, e.g.
56. Brown sugar?
58. Dope
59. Sale items: abbr.
60. Keepsake
61. Radio-controlled bomb
62. Week links
63. Contemptible type
64. Cry to a queue

DOWN

1. Spanish dance
2. Hooded plant
3. "Get — the Church on Time"
4. X-rated offering
5. Pristine
6. Sharp turn
7. Oodles
8. Campaign
9. — out (awaited anxiously)
10. Tuneful Shaw
11. Mendicant friars
12. Noted canal
13. Brief times
19. Ultimate
21. Suit, to Shakespeare

Solution is on page 218

24. Baby seal?

26. Eastwood's enforcer

28. Our, in Aix

29. Rubs it in

31. Mel and kin

32. Dams and does

33. Let slide

34. Ms. Cantrell

35. Cons' records

36. Cold sign

37. According to Gregor

44. Make — at (hit on)

45. Muppet raptor

47. Sherlock's addler?

48. Sarcastic

49. Honshu city

50. Hardly hurried

51. Island idol

53. *Trois et huit*

54. Sly as —

55. "Hands off!"

57. Japanese sect

19 LONG DIVISION

by Martin Ashwood-Smith

ACROSS

1. Fathomed
4. Had a bawl
8. Public show
12. *The Story* — (1975 blue movie)
13. Foundry employee
15. Maintain
16. Banking convenience: abbr.
17. Movie studio activity, at times
19. Macbeth title
21. W.S. Porter's nom
22. *Otto* lead-in
23. Flautist's kin
24. Beldam
27. New Agey pianist
29. Dramatic device
31. Capt.'s topper
32. Old alliance acronym
33. Peasant footwear
34. Peru neigh.
36. Franklin bill, slangily
38. Fabric ridge
39. Ricochets
41. Orrisroot extract
43. Alfonso's title
44. Silent, to Salieri
45. Scads
47. Malt brew
48. Order
50. Speech before dinner
52. Tam lines
53. Hailey bestseller
54. Skedaddles
58. Actress Claire
59. Lateral header
60. Alone
61. Antepenultimate mo.
62. Former JFK visitors
63. NASDAQ rival
64. Originally

DOWN

1. Fall guys
2. *The Day* — (Forsyth novel)
3. Bloody Mary base
4. Job trial?
5. Effect of going continental
6. Like the time before folks started dating
7. Surveillance accessories
8. Effortless
9. Sweet Roman age?
10. Con container
11. Assoc.

Solution is on page 218

13. Gloats

14. Artist Magritte

18. Tapestry town

20. Math degree?

24. Den doze

25. Troubled age

26. Magnate Jean Paul

28. Shamus

30. Aphorism

31. Hostess Perle

35. Human ancestor

37. Blew up: abbr.

40. March guy

42. Fourscore

46. Cortés quest

49. Mesozoic et al.

51. Tickle pink

52. One of these

54. Those chaps

55. Mental stats

56. Visceral

57. Land in *la mer*

by Eric Albert

ACROSS

1. Taper?
4. Old-fashioned one
8. Letter-perfect house?
14. Malt drink
15. Yuri's love
16. Lightly armed attack ship
17. Best Picture of 1937? (with "The")
20. Overshadow
21. Sax man Stan
22. Soon afterward
23. Hand-crossing time
25. *Carmina Burana* composer
29. Gender
30. Kander and Ebb show
33. Masseur's need
34. Speed checker
35. Overcome illness
37. Le Carré thriller?
41. It's built for two
42. Warrant
43. Wrong, notewise
44. Suit subject
47. Bad beginning?
50. Float on the breeze
52. Sharp spasm
53. Leap for Pavlova
54. Muffet buffet item
56. "Uh" equivalent
59. '79 name in the news?
63. Slide sight
64. Calliope, e.g.
65. *East of Eden* lad
66. Understood
67. Look of lust
68. Minnesota town

DOWN

1. Pressers and parkers
2. Platitude
3. Mirrored image
4. Fall flat
5. Oxen?
6. Packer place
7. Tasty tuber
8. Leblanc's Lupin
9. Wild and reckless
10. Hoffman role
11. Fuss
12. Alice's boss
13. Big time
18. Article in *Die Zeitung*
19. Hunchbacked helper
24. One in a shell
26. Go to the side
27. Register to run
28. Tied lure

Solution is on page 218

30. Surveyed larcenously

31. Sponsored messages

32. *Les — Mousquetaires*

34. Put down

36. Inclined

37. Long love seat

38. Hand warmer

39. She got married

40. Before, once

41. Intimidate

45. Missing link

46. Polite request

47. Threat

48. Lacking a key

49. With vulgarity

51. Bird call

53. Three in a row

55. Youthful deity

57. French flower

58. Person on a PC

59. Be "It"

60. Ins. plan

61. Balderdash

62. Size, briefly

by Dana Motley

ACROSS

1. Black Sea cottage
6. Horrify
11. Part of "TW3"
14. Historical circuit courts
15. Actor Greene
16. Clark's *Mogambo* costar
17. Start of the definition
19. First bone transplant?
20. Hole in the wall
21. Author of the definition
23. Rode a comber
26. Quarantine
27. Blue-ribbon
28. *Der Zauberberg* author
30. Flock females
31. Archaic maze header
32. Turner the thrush
33. Slump
35. Definition, Part 2
41. Lizzie Borden's feller
42. Curves
43. Dark event
44. 1 on Mohs' scale
47. *Gendarme*
48. Green fruit
49. Dilettante
52. Elder shunner
54. Definition, Part 3
56. 2,051 to Livy
57. Critic completer
58. End of the definition
62. End: prefix
63. "— Ben Jonson!"
64. Steamed state
65. Psyche parts
66. Church council
67. Takes ten

DOWN

1. Goddess, to Galba
2. Writer Rand
3. Buffet
4. Simple sugar
5. Beau tie
6. Wholly; quite
7. 11-Down native
8. Conductor André
9. Freud and Akhmatova
10. "And when I ope my lips — dog bark!" (Shakespeare)
11. City on the Vistula
12. Emulate Yeager
13. Buffalo icemen
18. Religious recluse
22. Mournful opus
23. Sontag subject

Solution is on page 219

24. Stir

25. Linda of soaps

29. Oboelike

32. A Ritter

33. Yield

34. Paid spots

36. Saguaros, e.g.

37. Noted Speaker

38. British tea maker

39. *Protocol* star

40. Assam silkworm

44. Gauguin's getaway

45. Wowed

46. Stereotypes

47. Hayward role

48. Slugger Al

50. Moral nature

51. Shark's sin

53. Vilify

55. Casino game

59. Composer Rorem

60. Fetch

61. Elders: abbr.

by Eric Albert

ACROSS

1. '70s sitcom
5. Put aside
9. Move like an owl
14. Concept
15. Devilish delight
16. Sure of succeeding
17. Sate
18. Mexican peninsula
19. Give off
20. Inanity
23. Singer Sumac
24. Alien org.
25. He gets what's coming to him
26. Yeast drink
27. "Back in Black" rockers
28. Survey
31. Marsh bird
34. "By Jove!"
35. High desert
36. Transmission ender?
39. Claim to be
40. Be a monger
41. Third planet
42. Ask for alms
43. Source
44. *Hedera helix*
45. Decorative molding
46. Highland pronoun
47. Raincoat
50. Lincoln memorial?
54. First wirer
55. Babe in the woods
56. Singer James
57. Morticia's man
58. Hence
59. Autocrat
60. Body politic
61. Masculine principle
62. Celtic church

DOWN

1. Two score and ten
2. Characteristic style
3. Alabama town
4. Partial
5. Fillet
6. Squashed circles
7. Suva's locale
8. Drilling aid
9. Fine for photographing
10. Floor tool
11. Responsibility
12. Tout's info
13. "Tintinnabulation" user
21. Refueling vessel
22. Gabler with grit
26. Once more
27. Bond, e.g.
28. Wild waste
29. Touch (upon)

Solution is on page 219

30. Heart of the matter
31. Complain peevishly
32. Wander about
33. Fascinated
34. Tossup
35. Aussie "hi"
37. Eggish

38. Worse than late?
43. Stand like a statue
44. Bewildered
45. Show shower
46. Straighten
47. Gaynor of *South Pacific*
48. Marriage spot

49. Rhett player
50. Pay, as a bill
51. *The Joy of Cooking* author Rombauer
52. Yuri's love
53. Call's mate
54. RDA units

by Lois Sidway

ACROSS

1. Wild celebration
5. Make the sparks fly
9. Test type
13. Aleutian outpost
14. Subject of Jason's betrayal
15. Science series
16. Straight
17. Lets up
18. Hidden valley
19. Clayton Moore costar
22. Mantra murmurs
23. Seasonal song
24. Pronoun for Pierrette
25. Pet rocks, e.g.
26. Time of your life?
27. Crow hello
30. Pre-Lenten fete
34. Lay hands (on)
36. Mete (out)
37. Culp sidekick
39. Major party
40. Host
42. Eleanor's uncle
44. Negative
45. Neckline shape
47. Grable display
48. Oscar winner Jannings
50. Grad
52. Somewhat: suffix
55. Gene Autry sidekick
58. Dirty
59. Score, in Paris
60. Mitchell's manse
61. Artist Bonheur
62. Fencing tools
63. Quick blow
64. Urgent abbr.
65. Jerk
66. Darkroom dip

DOWN

1. Seeger strings
2. First-string group
3. Doesn't raise
4. Crude abodes
5. Emulate Marner
6. A Ford
7. Lecherous look
8. Sprint expert
9. Pinhead hoofer?
10. Philatelist or numismatist
11. Composer Charles
12. Bestselling Brown
14. Tuneful
20. — instant
21. Line to the Sinai
25. Untrammeled

Solution is on page 219

26. Czech river
28. Farm unit
29. Tot's query
30. Torpor
31. Jonson play subject
32. Use citizen power
33. Souvenir of an old flame
35. Energy source
36. Study
38. Dairy buys
41. Satanic specialty
43. Curse
46. Time for tea
49. Sforza center
50. A Doubleday
51. Slid for gold
52. Site of 49-Down
53. Ready to paint
54. "It takes a — livin'…"
55. Flue filler
56. Cry of pain
57. Engrave
58. *Mme.*, to Juan

by Matt Gaffney

ACROSS

1. Vertical construction
5. Price setting?
10. Mike's adjunct
13. Nephew of Cain
14. Marine
15. Fan noise
16. Refuse to budge
18. Before, to Browning
19. Scandinavians in Moscow
20. Lifts, of a sort
21. Tower svc.
22. Wanting in completeness
25. Casebook entries
27. Cry, cry again
28. Depth charger?
31. Farewell from Hilo
32. Big pic.
34. Displayed dependence
36. Deviate
40. High-class café
41. Haloed woman, briefly
42. Galley goofs
43. Bengals' org.
45. Has the last word
48. Los Angeles layers
49. Atlantic food fish
52. Actor Chaney
53. Atoll builder
56. Miss Piggy's pronoun
57. Mined-over matter
58. Demonstrates
61. Gun's offspring?
62. Have a meeting of minds
63. Last Stuart
64. Quarry blaster
65. Passes out in play
66. Some summer neonates

DOWN

1. Richelieu's rug
2. ASAP
3. Lea sound
4. Rome direction
5. Cyclopean trademark
6. Peaked
7. Sinister
8. Also-—— (losers)
9. Malt treat
10. Washington's is 202
11. Benoit's event
12. Plumed game
16. Wellness wkrs.
17. RMN challenger
23. Kermit ——
24. Tell all

Solution is on page 219

25. Swooned

26. "— in his own time"

29. The — Good Feeling

30. Hinder

33. Alamos lead-in

35. Refrains from singing?

36. Takes a wrong turn

37. Sweet sorrow, e.g.

38. Foe

39. D.C. code crackers

44. Tracks

46. Masker's wear

47. Tea cakes

50. Wing

51. Young fox

53. Canary condo

54. Gumbo pod

55. Wintle

58. Seeing red

59. Crony

60. Basic bill

by Martin Ashwood-Smith

ACROSS

1. Posse's pursuit
10. Corrupted
15. Turned on
16. Hole — (ace)
17. Start of a Goethe quotation
18. Role for Rita
19. Mafia chief
20. He's full of sound and phooey
21. Dead ducks
22. Spanish region
24. "No man might buy —…" (Revelation)
26. Group status
27. Ford scion
29. Carioca's home
30. — Z
31. Varnish ingredient
33. Stable grain
34. HRE leader
35. Middle of the quotation
40. Stout houses
41. Calamity
42. Chinese dynasty
43. Honored few of WWII
44. In the cards
45. Flows from
49. Annex
50. Soothe
54. Church records
55. Facing forward
57. Tibetan gazelles
59. In public
60. Two quartets
61. End of the quotation
63. Amusing Martin
64. Shower of stars?
65. Seuss trio
66. Austerity

DOWN

1. Loaf
2. Reported back?
3. Pros with pads
4. Safety device?
5. Maliciously sinning
6. Ham's medium
7. It's often shed
8. Significant others
9. Shakespearean expletives
10. Paid dance partner
11. Getting — years
12. Stomach
13. Mario of motor racing
14. Sugar measure
21. Bug

Solution is on page 220

23. Carter and Gwyn

25. Hunks of history

28. Appealing activity?

32. Corral

33. Sapphic stanzas

34. "— vincit amor" (Virgil)

35. It goes to blazes

36. Selected sayings

37. Puffs up

38. College drill gp.

39. Gig guider

44. Digs

46. Bracket light

47. Chopin showstoppers

48. Pan et al.

51. Booker

52. Michaels of "SNL"

53. City jefe

56. Kline film

58. Avoid

61. Body duct

62. Abby's sister

by Paul Matwychuk

ACROSS

1. These, in Toulon
4. Comment from a bridge player
9. Navigators Islands, today
14. Crossword cuckoo
15. Rich dessert
16. Hair weave
17. Compass point
18. Limpid
19. Usher's beat
20. Migraines
23. Metallic mixture
24. Stadium standard
27. Actor Roger
28. Church levy
31. Malarial symptom
32. Investment procedure?
33. Agenda entries
34. Wash and wear, e.g.
40. Privileged ones
41. Danielle's dream
42. From scratch
43. Falsify
45. Dern's mom
49. Smith who embraced Big Brother
51. Site
52. *Revolution From Within* writer
56. Earn a ticket
58. Daub
59. Spenser lady
60. Mil. acronym
61. Foreshadowings
62. Hoofer Miller
63. Hazardous
64. Hailing from Oslo
65. Would-be gent

DOWN

1. Rubicon crosser
2. Save your fodder
3. Age, in Arles
4. Restless
5. Flag waver?
6. Field
7. South African town
8. Angelic figure
9. Hall-of-Famer Warren
10. Estrange
11. Delts manipulator
12. Artistic medium
13. Bolted down
21. Greek isle
22. Calendar opener?
25. Frozen
26. Her Angel abandoned her
28. Randy's rinkmate

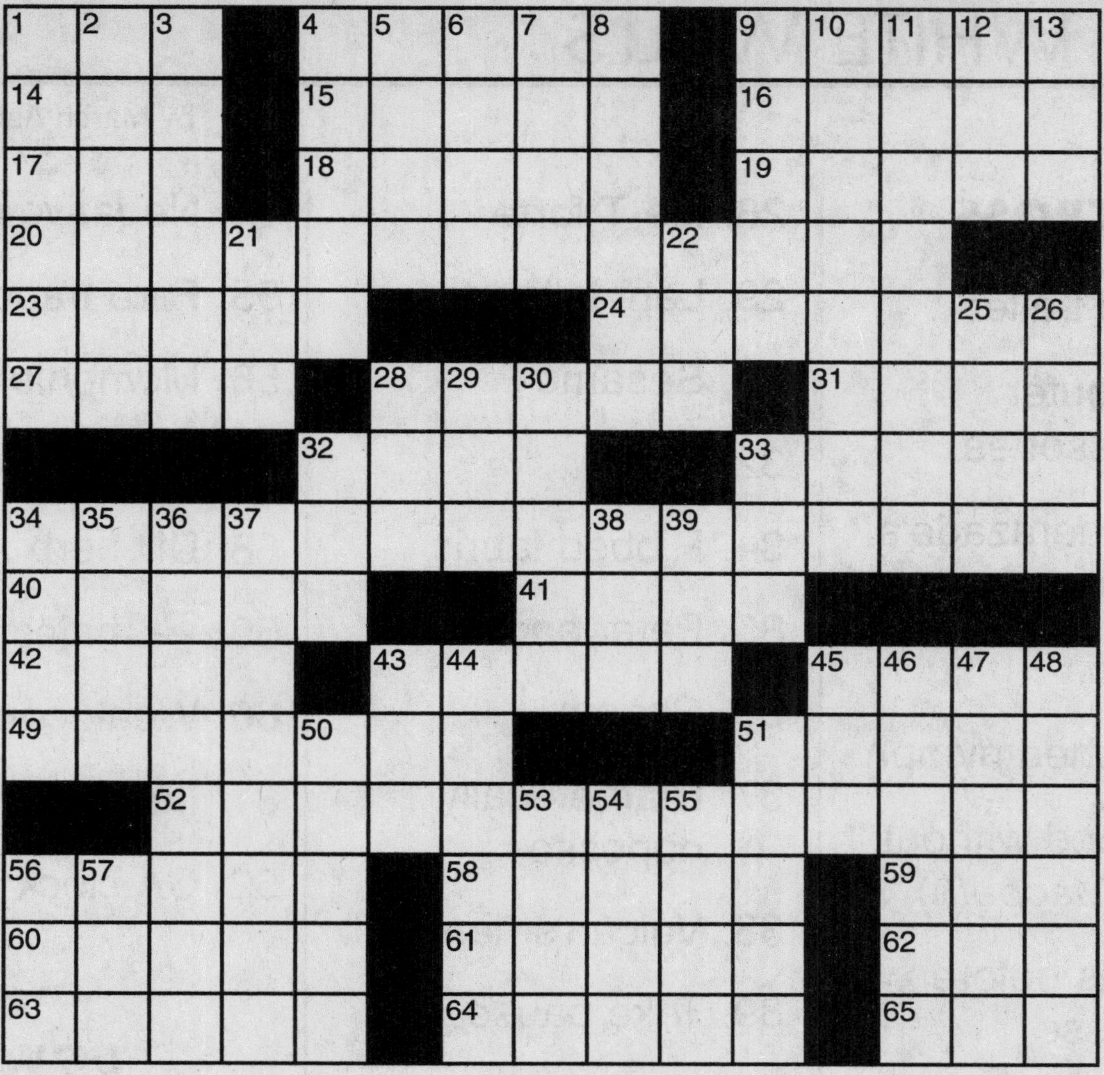
1
2
3
4
5
6
7
8
9
10
11
12
13
14
15
16
17
18
19
20
21
22
23
24
25
26
27
28
29
30
31
32
33
34
35
36
37
38
39
40
41
42
43
44
45
46
47
48
49
50
51
52
53
54
55
56
57
58
59
60
61
62
63
64
65

Solution is on page 220

29. Addams cousin
30. Show place?
32. Defunct spy org.
33. Personal contraction
34. Warm time
35. Hindu royal
36. Score levelers
37. Paper feeder?
38. Brit's greens
39. Aide to Margo
43. Supporting
44. Synchronicity
45. Floral wreath
46. Like the Oscars
47. Chaperon
48. Supply temperer
50. Hot potable
51. Ballad bit
53. Shot or shell
54. Sign reader
55. Sun shades
56. H.S. elder
57. Luau staple

27 WHITE WALLS

by Martin Ashwood-Smith

ACROSS

1. Henri trailer
5. Computer accessories
9. Scheherazade's residence
14. Bereft
15. Vanished nymph
16. "A deed without —" (*Macbeth*)
17. Words before impasse
18. Sewer's oath?
19. V-shaped fortification
20. Leu fractions
21. Single: prefix
22. Lamentation
23. Ole and Merlin
25. Come down after a lift?
27. Portuguese cape
28. Ice-T forte
29. Lent follower
31. Sesame
32. Tars
34. Ribbed fabric
35. Peter and Paul
36. Chasm
37. Diametrically opposite
38. Vulcan's hangout
39. Take pause
41. Morse click
42. Aristocratic types
43. Canine command
44. Alfonso's queen et al.
46. Naval agreements
47. Heater
49. Spot checker?
51. Make a run for it
53. Pen residents
54. Negative particle
55. Fare trader
56. Memphis bull
57. Image: prefix
58. Dill herb
59. — majesty
60. Weak consonants
61. Inactive
62. CA clock settings

DOWN

1. Nit-picker's métier
2. Nation's advocacy
3. Tissue grafting, e.g.
4. Ward of Warbucks
5. Jellyfish specimens
6. Personal pep talk?
7. Indian Ocean body

Solution is on page 220

8. Old age group?

9. Feather barb

10. It's loaned by a listener

11. Big dishes

12. Freedom fighter

13. Cerebral activities

22. Quill

24. Loch in the Caledonian Canal

26. "No returns, please!"

30. With wisdom

33. Chapter in history

34. Putrefy

37. — *doble* (music for matadors)

39. Get wind (of)

40. Wood worker?

45. Stood out

48. Pate wrap

50. Slugger Slaughter

52. Rink leap

55. Asian people

by Wilma Schulman

ACROSS

1. Canine complaints
5. What to take from the stage
9. Groom with care
14. Exhortation to action
15. *Jewel in the Crown*'s Kumar
16. À la King?
17. Paul Scofield epic
20. Henry the carver
21. Look of lust
22. Within: prefix
23. Not stereo
25. Stir violently
27. Jazz singer Anita
30. Ten from Sinai
35. Millennium div.
36. O'Neill's offspring
37. Reward for applause
38. Cipher clerk
40. RR terminus
42. Mink's aquatic kin
43. Astronomy Muse
45. French state
47. Chang's close connection
48. Peck vacation pic
50. Ferrara family
51. Indigo dye
52. Cooper costar
54. Kin group
57. Current abbr.
59. High camp?
63. Michael Douglas flick
66. Birch tree
67. Sufficient, for bards
68. Pre-Nadia Olympic pixie
69. Skater's edge
70. Vetch weed
71. Bird's cane item

DOWN

1. Garden party?
2. Hard cheese
3. Fum header
4. Turbulent
5. "Gotcha!"
6. Airy fliers
7. Heraldic border
8. Sager sage
9. Fabled bed bump
10. Choose again
11. Pressing item
12. Matter topper
13. Manila moola
18. Vintage car
19. Wear away
24. Sgt., for one
26. — *Rappaport*
27. Happen

Solution is on page 220

28. Rio — (African territory)

29. Nicobar's mate

31. Beat Boris or Bobby

32. Heeds

33. Ontario river

34. Lint magnet

36. Belted hunter

39. Souped up

41. Moored

44. Ripley's enemy

46. Salty endorsement

49. — *By* (Steve Allen film)

50. Joy bringer

53. Spots; plugs

54. Sourpuss

55. Lounge about

56. Williams matriarch

58. Lab burner

60. Small rodent

61. *Picnic* penner

62. Out of power

64. Fury

65. Ram's dam

29 TRIPLETS

by Andrew Rowan

ACROSS

1. Cooperate, criminally
11. Glass snake, e.g.
15. Fixed
16. Be nomadic
17. A crying shame
18. He's always in "Jeopardy!"
19. Ladies' room?
20. Eldritch
21. Play the coquette
22. Call box
24. Jai alai implement
26. Ayesha the eternal
27. Sightseers
28. High degree?: abbr.
29. More like Croesus
31. Colombian metropolis
33. Men on mounds
34. Gives goose bumps
36. Gaping
37. Fire on from hiding
38. Like-not link
39. White-sale purchases
40. Prize (apart)
41. Latin being
45. Darwinian's ancestor
46. Moral man
48. Playful aquatic animal
49. Ankle gaiters
51. Hecuba's husband
53. Old Japanese coin
54. "For — jolly…"
55. Interpret verbatim
57. Famed Roman reproach
58. Polygraph pads
59. Reddens, maybe
60. Cardiovascular assessment

DOWN

1. Inclined
2. Call — (quit)
3. Do harm
4. Had a little beef
5. Gold seeker, briefly
6. Spoil (with "on")
7. Rebel of a sort
8. Coddled
9. Gardner namesakes
10. Nautical chain
11. Central Asian sea
12. Abrasive one?
13. "This way!"

Solution is on page 221

14. Sinisters' opposites

21. — middling

23. POW's plan

25. Con with clout

28. Tickle pink

30. Bordeaux export

32. Fan belts?

33. Temporary locks

34. Short-tempered

35. Film aficionado

37. Pruned prices

40. Grip grabber

42. Take steps

43. Confiscates

44. Literary Dowson

47. Slopped over

48. Sharif and Bradley

50. Crosses of antiquity

52. Wiles

55. Avignon article

56. Parcel

by Alex Vaughn

ACROSS

1. Rural mouthful
5. Grow less aloof
9. Overconfident
14. Mimetic bird
15. Blush wine
16. Layer in trouble
17. Glancing reference?
20. See 19-Down
21. Greek letters
22. Dieters' surpluses: abbr.
23. Hardy heroine
25. Biblical verb
27. Mustang coll.
30. Mild expletive
32. Tryst invitation
36. Cuff ornament
38. Sluggish black rail
40. Shakespearean sprite
41. Perfume shop?
44. Relatives of crêpes
45. Scissorhands portrayer
46. Old Stoic
47. Gender bias
49. Spotted
51. Equivalent wd.
52. GI's DIs, e.g.
54. Lose it
56. Towards the fantail
59. It has it?
61. Noisy skirmish
65. Play touch football?
68. Hawaiian island
69. Betrayer of 23-Across
70. Opera wrap
71. Revise
72. North Sea feeder
73. Pan's foe

DOWN

1. Laconic wheedle
2. Publicity
3. Prime the pot
4. Trouser spec
5. Do, as business
6. Total: prefix
7. PDQ
8. Llandudno language
9. *Mer* man
10. Pts. of 22-Across
11. Entwine
12. Bulbous bulge
13. Cravings
18. Campus colleen
19. With 20-Across, *Darkman* actor
24. Lock holder
26. Frequency unit

Solution is on page 221

27. Slovenly ones

28. Thousand

29. Disengage

31. Sail inserts

33. They hit the roof

34. Eeny follower

35. Showy John

37. Gordon's guy

39. A and O

42. TV oater hero

43. Sandwich variety

48. — *Lisa*

50. DEA officer

53. Legislators *à Paris*

55. Mend

56. Fit

57. Drum beat

58. Color quality

60. In vain

62. *Goodbye, Columbus*

63. Cycle competitor

64. Hide's mate

66. Fire

67. Sawbuck

by Michael Selinker

ACROSS

1. Social climber's goal
10. IMPS expansion
12. LENS expansion
14. Stimpy's pal
15. Short-necked diving bird
16. Red suit
18. Vichy export, in Madrid
20. PhD and MSc, for two
23. Scans, in a way
24. Canio's love
26. Like a perfect game
28. Urban transports
29. Host components
31. Wilder title opening
32. Cakes' companion
33. RODE expansion
36. Moving sight?
38. Oinker
39. Pied Piper: rats::St. Patrick: —
43. Financial help
44. Palindromic flights
46. Aussie canine
47. Impassive
49. Change clues, e.g.
51. Latvian gulf
52. Town near Luxor
54. Bikini part
56. In place of
57. LINES expansion
61. DARES expansion
62. *Gulliver's Travels* star

DOWN

1. Solder metal
2. Tasmanian peak
3. Pen name: abbr.
4. Soft and lustrous
5. Literary monogram
6. Idiot
7. 1942 Marjorie Main comedy
8. On deck
9. Grass blade
10. Small, to Juan
11. Acre land
12. Silver Bullet Band leader
13. Gnomon
14. Go nuts
17. They've been through a couple of rough drafts: abbr.
19. Decorate
21. DOG expansion
22. Actor Andrew

Solution is on page 221

25. Mimic

27. Sale find: abbr.

30. NYC district

32. Oil-well capper Red

34. Opera part

35. Wrap up

36. Essential

37. Groupie

40. Wounds with a shiv

41. Incite

42. Take wing

43. Supplicate

44. Ladder, to Livy

45. Although, in Acapulco

48. Atlas feature

50. Lock

53. Famed pirate

55. And more

58. Kookie Byrnes of TV

59. Brady bill foes

60. Hokkaido coin

by Joel Hess

ACROSS

1. City of 21-Down
5. First victim
9. Tennis surface, sometimes
14. Diving bird
15. Staff sight
16. Grimm characters
17. Blind part
18. Absorbed with
19. Detaches over time
20. Figurinelike?
23. Teachers' org.
24. Chamorro's predecessor
28. Wore out the rug
32. Footnote abbr.
35. Stick starter?
36. Maine park
38. Muhammad's cousin
39. Smell — (get bad vibes)
40. Looks that could kill?
43. Shine's partner
44. — polloi
45. "Hurrah!"
46. Actress Claire
47. Manco Capac's people
49. Librarian's gadget
50. Signed the deal
53. August sign
55. Like Finland?
62. Wrangles
65. Grain spikes
66. Avatar of Vishnu
67. Noted Palmer, to pals
68. Pampas avian
69. Bulb bloom
70. Runway figure
71. Crooner Vallee
72. Breton, e.g.

DOWN

1. Moreover
2. Couples' game
3. Be peripatetic
4. Feed the kitty
5. Ouzo spice
6. Kin to ikebana
7. Wagon train?
8. Iberian realm
9. Minaret, for example
10. Catalyst
11. Women's wear daily?
12. Author Deighton
13. Tight turn
21. Sari state?
22. Make changes
25. Totally absorbed
26. Chin warmer
27. Pollen holder
28. Fatherland, to Nero

Solution is on page 221

29. Sore

30. Cleo's first love

31. Sidle

33. Programming language

34. UN agency

37. They secrete honeydew

39. *Un angelo*'s strings

41. Lo-o-o-ng time

42. Anne Hathaway, in 1616

48. Great Brit?

51. Unearthly

52. Studio stand

54. Lamb product

56. VI or GU

57. Hawaiian isle

58. Idle fellow?

59. Challenge

60. Author Ludwig

61. Democratic donkey creator

62. Bible bk.

63. Expert

64. Furthermore

by Bob Sefick

ACROSS

1. Miss Piggy's date?
5. Put away
9. Hissing sound
12. Greek leather flasks
14. Deck at Shea
15. Interstate mover
16. Children's book by Katherine Oana
18. Express approval
19. Got the better of
20. Underling
22. Far-out visitor
23. Couldn't swallow
25. Lode of ore
27. Loser's cry
28. Level
31. Reputation
33. Turn off
36. Start of a life sentence?
37. Sheepskin coat
39. Seine holm
40. Bolivian lake
42. *Bus Stop* penner
43. Break
44. Caledonian coins
46. Peru pronoun
48. Go over
51. Violinist Morini
54. Caesar's cloak
55. Aromatic
58. "— it" (amen)
59. Zoroastrian scriptures
61. Common rubber-stamp word
62. Ashtabula's lakefront
63. Log
64. Immobile: abbr.
65. Witnessed
66. Georgia county

DOWN

1. Foolish one
2. Batting champ Tony
3. Fencing move: French
4. Play again
5. Part of a quarter note
6. Tyrrhenian Sea feeder
7. Key word
8. Bony marine fish
9. Insane jealousy
10. PR pro's concern
11. Played the syrinx
13. Fine, uncoined silver
15. Candle holder
17. Hindu harem: var.
21. — incognita
24. Leave the cocoon

Solution is on page 222

26. Eisenhower and Van Doren

28. Put down

29. Hubbub

30. Dread of animals

32. Chess piece

34. Shade tree

35. Sheltered side

37. In a belt

38. Grayish green

41. Broke cover?

43. Conclusion

45. Passing manias

47. Rich haul

48. Grates

49. WWII craft

50. Pyle or Banks

52. Jai alai catcher

53. Fed the pot

56. Garden spot

57. Vetch weed

60. Afore

by Louis Sabin

ACROSS

1. Tocsin
6. Coptic bishop
10. Vacationing
14. *As You Like It* lass
15. Limerick master
16. Ole Miss rival
17. Screen mouse
20. Standing
21. Appended number
22. Styx ferryman
25. Change clothes?
26. Acted like 39-Across
27. Quebec peninsula
30. At times it's rare
35. Buck ender
37. Ginza glow
38. Buccaneers' venue
39. Song mouse

42. Bench, in 43-Across
43. Piedmont commune
44. Silent Negri
45. Stage direction
46. Comedian's slippers?
48. Clutch of eggs
49. Take to court
51. Certain believers
53. Refuge
57. Wizard
59. Mickey Mouse flick
64. Fill with oakum
65. Norse opus
66. Doubtful
67. Promote with zeal
68. Lively dance
69. Cancel

DOWN

1. Bank record: abbr.
2. Summer sign
3. Freddy's street
4. Closer to fruition
5. Director Norman
6. Evelyn's brother
7. Actor Lahr
8. Echolocation master
9. Marshal
10. Letter group
11. Storm path
12. Grace closer
13. Sale site, sometimes
18. Vassal
19. "— Fideles"
22. Tarzan player
23. Chief Justice Stone
24. Rub oil on

Solution is on page 222

25. Betoken

28. Pancho's poncho

29. Equilibrium

31. Drive down

32. Make a cameo, e.g.

33. Young chimp

34. Jeweler's units

36. Former

40. Back

41. Leather coat?

47. Way past one's prime

50. Earth tone

52. Lazybones

53. Author Sholem

54. Kennel order

55. Pained cry

56. Tarn

57. Golf slice

58. Font choice: abbr.

60. Keats forte

61. Pasture

62. 1040 harvester

63. Storm heart

by Harvey Estes

ACROSS

1. Lovers' miff
5. Letter from a sweetheart?
10. Unruly ruler?
13. *The Mephisto Waltz* star
14. Improvised
15. Lone soaring
16. Chops provider
17. Bambi persecutes?
19. Cash holder
21. Had a hero
22. Funny folks
23. Morning fare
25. Assignment
27. Stretch the truth
28. Travel org.
29. Fade to black
31. Backbones of families
32. Chi hoopster follows closely?
34. Plains tribe
36. Coolers
37. Sullen
38. M. Matisse
40. Volkswagen carries?
44. Sweet tubers
45. Nonentities
47. Long March leader
48. Rocky peak
49. Fictional sub captain
50. Use a menu
52. Legible
54. Ger. auto
56. Wear out
57. Pegasus does his thing?
60. New Zealander
62. Ark groups
63. Executed again
64. "Heavens!"
65. Lith. was one
66. Auguries
67. Vegan staple

DOWN

1. Paul's *Exodus* costar
2. Period of no growth
3. Ito's rank
4. Put aside
5. Tear-jerking
6. Muse's bestowal
7. Urban enclaves
8. Wells' mad scientist
9. Köln cry
10. Leno specialty
11. Retro
12. Tweed et al.
15. — generis
18. Home for Mindy's guy
20. Eloper's aid

Solution is on page 222

23. Truck part
24. Give a roar of approval?
26. Straight men
30. Metric amounts: abbr.
31. Paddock parent
33. Hosp. workers
35. Even numbers, vis-à-vis integers
37. Pair
38. Consecrates
39. Penguin variety
40. Dull saw
41. Vespucci of note
42. Drag, at times
43. Tosspot
44. Olympic vehicles
46. Flag, e.g.
49. Compass point
51. Is partial to
53. Onager
55. Moselle quaff
58. To's partner
59. Radical '60s org.
61. Ms. Lupino

by Manny Nosowsky

ACROSS

1. Tap for sap
6. Thumb-pinkie gap
10. Quondam
14. Fax forerunner
15. "Blue Moon" lyricist
16. County capital
17. Derelict in one's duty?
20. Part of a perfect game
21. — *Giant Shadow*
22. Ape's cousin
25. Feminine cosmological principle
26. Beset
30. Crooked
32. Restaurateur Shor
33. Spread out
35. DA's aide
39. Advice for one in denial?
42. Step, in Sonora
43. Unit for Ben and Jerry
44. — up-and-up
45. Eschew
47. In flourishing fashion
48. Jeff Davis supporter
51. Part of a full house
54. Uniform
56. Mighty Duck blast
61. Bonkers?
64. Long-tailed flier
65. Lox, stock and bagel joint
66. Was part of a '60s protest
67. Receptive
68. Woman, to Nathan Detroit
69. Knight ride

DOWN

1. Hindu follower?
2. Chihuahua coin
3. *Winnie — Pu*
4. Creep's peep
5. Practice
6. Punctually
7. Scapegoat
8. Kahlo output
9. Utmost degree
10. Greek peak
11. Full of gossip
12. Jumping chollas, e.g.
13. Green Mountain Allen
18. Combine
19. Outer: prefix
23. Youngest son
24. First Hebrew letter
26. "Take — from me"
27. Dagwood's spot
28. Hooch hounds
29. Friend of D'Artagnan
31. Dupes

Solution is on page 222

33. High-pitched complaint
34. Tennis coach Tiriac
36. Horologist Thomas
37. *Heartland* author
38. Die side with three pips
40. Twirled or whirled
41. Grouch

46. Robin's first word
47. Ananias
48. Arkady — (Smith's sleuth)
49. Set up
50. Isolated hill
52. "Miserere," for one
53. Caine's philandering Cockney

55. Egyptian deity
57. "Get lost!"
58. Abhor
59. Any Dust Bowl victim
60. Shepherd
62. Sum up
63. Swell place?

by Bob Sefick

ACROSS

1. You might have a few at a barbecue
10. Bloke
14. Mail carrier?
15. Form
16. Subpoenas
17. Buccaneers' base
18. Cold spell
19. Tribe of Israel
20. With decorum
21. Maternal relations
23. Event for the beau monde
24. Needlefish
25. Break up
27. Doctor's device
30. Tessera
31. Post-holiday resolution
32. Alfonso's consort
33. Spread throughout

36. Singles bar?
37. Money dispensers: abbr.
39. Litigates
40. Hungarian sister
42. Academic division
44. Fighting word for Fido
45. *One of Ours* was one of hers
46. Props of a sort
49. Wodehouse's Wooster
50. Giant word for Jack?
51. Limerick land
53. Allan-—— (Hood hood)
54. Remarked
56. Focused
57. Maryland was one
58. Outdated map ltrs.
59. Speaks to

DOWN

1. Lip
2. Desiccated edible
3. Mideast capital
4. Spree
5. Tokyo, once
6. Carnival confederate
7. Rick's beloved et al.
8. Worked on brakes
9. Letters from Gilligan's Island?
10. Presided
11. Setting up board meetings?
12. Chapman's moniker
13. Austin —— University
15. Section
20. Dissembled
22. Camden Yards' cover

Solution is on page 223

23. First name in Raveloe

25. Auk or grebe

26. Singing James

27. Shooter ammo

28. Comes before

29. Penetrating photons

30. More faithful

34. Helena rival

35. Painter Nolde

38. Mediator

41. Stresses

43. Recoiled

44. Column checker

46. Saw red

47. Hayworth and Rudner

48. Rough ridge

49. Azerbaijan capital

50. Mustang, for one

52. Greek resistance gp.

54. University gridiron gp.

55. Chin attachment?

by Ernie Furtado

ACROSS

1. Relative of PDQ
5. Roo moves
10. — *facto*
14. Goodman's old costar
15. "Dallas" matriarch
16. Thurmond or Archibald
17. Wings
18. Ski terrain
19. Slavic sovereign
20. Whalebone
23. Amherst sch.
24. Is ambitious
27. Movie location
28. Spanker or spinnaker
32. Spellbound
33. Funny bone
36. It's on the tip of his Tung
38. Championship
39. Surface for Witt
40. Soup bones
43. Declaim
44. — importance (trifling)
45. Ref. book
48. Finery
51. Danny's daughter
53. Wishbone
57. A crowd, in Wiesbaden
59. Covered courtyards
60. Tipple
61. Different, to Don Juan
62. Deciphers
63. The way the wind blows
64. Org.
65. German expressionist Max
66. Cincinnati nine

DOWN

1. Beaded calculator
2. Strauss opera
3. Ark landfall
4. It always makes headlines
5. "— we forget"
6. Quoins
7. Diamond family name
8. Browning's "— Passes"
9. Oozes
10. Machinations
11. Hot stuff from the deli
12. B & O stop
13. Complete, to Keats
21. Start of NC's motto
22. Flashy fish
25. Group of heroic poems

Solution is on page 223

26. Fr. Dowling discourse
29. Con
30. "...pudding — the eating"
31. Unhand
33. Parochial
34. Royal Norse name
35. Nonflowering plant
36. Spare in the trunk
37. Walks a crooked line
40. — favor, Señor
41. Port preceder
42. NYC cultural mecca
45. Baltimore bird
46. Eschewed the formalities
47. Receivers
49. "Do — to eat a peach?"
50. Following
52. — of roses
54. Algerian seaport
55. Frees, in a way
56. Spar
57. Film noir classic
58. NFL linemen

by Alex Vaughn

ACROSS

1. Little man blue?
6. Crude controllers
10. Sidewise scuttler
14. Evangelist's name meaning "beloved"
15. Sex guru Dr. —
16. Help ham get better?
17. Be obviously lost
20. *Soigné*
21. Author Hong Kingston
22. Pharm. watchdog
25. Swing and miss
26. Cave, at times
27. Unforgettable Cole
28. Tolkien's Frodo
32. — cuss
33. Subside
34. Member of a pressure group
35. Patron's passion
36. Made tracks
40. Noted cowgirl
43. Iran had a peacock one
45. Hits every nightspot
48. Phony beginning?
49. School in Troy, NY
50. Stage in putting on of pants
51. Check around
52. Andre of Opens
54. Was just terrible
56. Enthusiastic bet
61. Home of Rama, amah, Brahma and lama
62. Pliny's path
63. Old-photo tone
64. Robust muscle
65. Sci-fi sub skipper
66. Patrick of roundball

DOWN

1. Acknowledged that the anthem was over
2. Famous space station
3. Actress Thurman
4. Makes a rod roar
5. Sympathize with
6. Carol kings source
7. Purple-haired, maybe
8. Et al. cousin
9. Phantasm
10. Metellus Cimber's 310
11. Supreme Court dictum
12. Where varsities vie
13. Assailed by ills
18. Like spinach
19. — up the flagpole (proposed an idea)
22. Sprawl suddenly
23. Bible illustrator
24. Composer Thomas
26. One is national

Solution is on page 223

29. *Tarzan, the Ape Man* director
30. Raspy-sounding
31. Jawaharlal, for one
35. In opposition to
37. Inner Hebrides isle
38. Means justifiers
39. Registration area

41. Pursuer of vice?
42. "Childproof cap" stuff
43. Bald tire's lack
44. Harmless snake type
45. "Yikes!"
46. Charlotte —, V.I.
47. The Pamplona underdog

48. '70s peacemaker
53. Deli dish
54. Staunch
55. Had acquaintance with
57. Marie, e.g.
58. Ltrs. with a dateline
59. Pewter component
60. Yield to gravity

by Martin Ashwood-Smith

ACROSS

1. Charles I's architect
11. Like avian elevators
15. Darwin was one
16. Compos mentis
17. Monthly mailings
18. Make tracks?
19. Field yield
20. Anathema
21. Squibs
22. Hi's partner
24. Month after Adar
26. Dig in
27. Refer ender
28. Canticle
29. Laconian city
31. Ranch guests
33. More like a couch potato
34. Thalberg's wife
37. Most saucy
38. Court activity
39. Mount Ida's island
40. Pretend to be
41. Moo man of the comics
42. Burn the midnight oil
46. Ordinal ending
47. Doesn't own
49. Botanical bristle
50. Fork-tailed gulls
52. Plenty, previously
54. May, for sure
55. Ms. Brickell
56. Scientist of a sort
59. Mysterious character
60. Perry of the theater
61. Went like the wind
62. Cassette's cousin

DOWN

1. Oxford area
2. Prohibition promoter
3. Boldface alternative
4. Like some reactions
5. Look for it in vein
6. Door frame post
7. Dogbane relative
8. Dumbbells
9. Kefauver of the Senate crime committee
10. Ave. intersectors
11. Diminutive deputy?
12. View from Toledo
13. Sparks

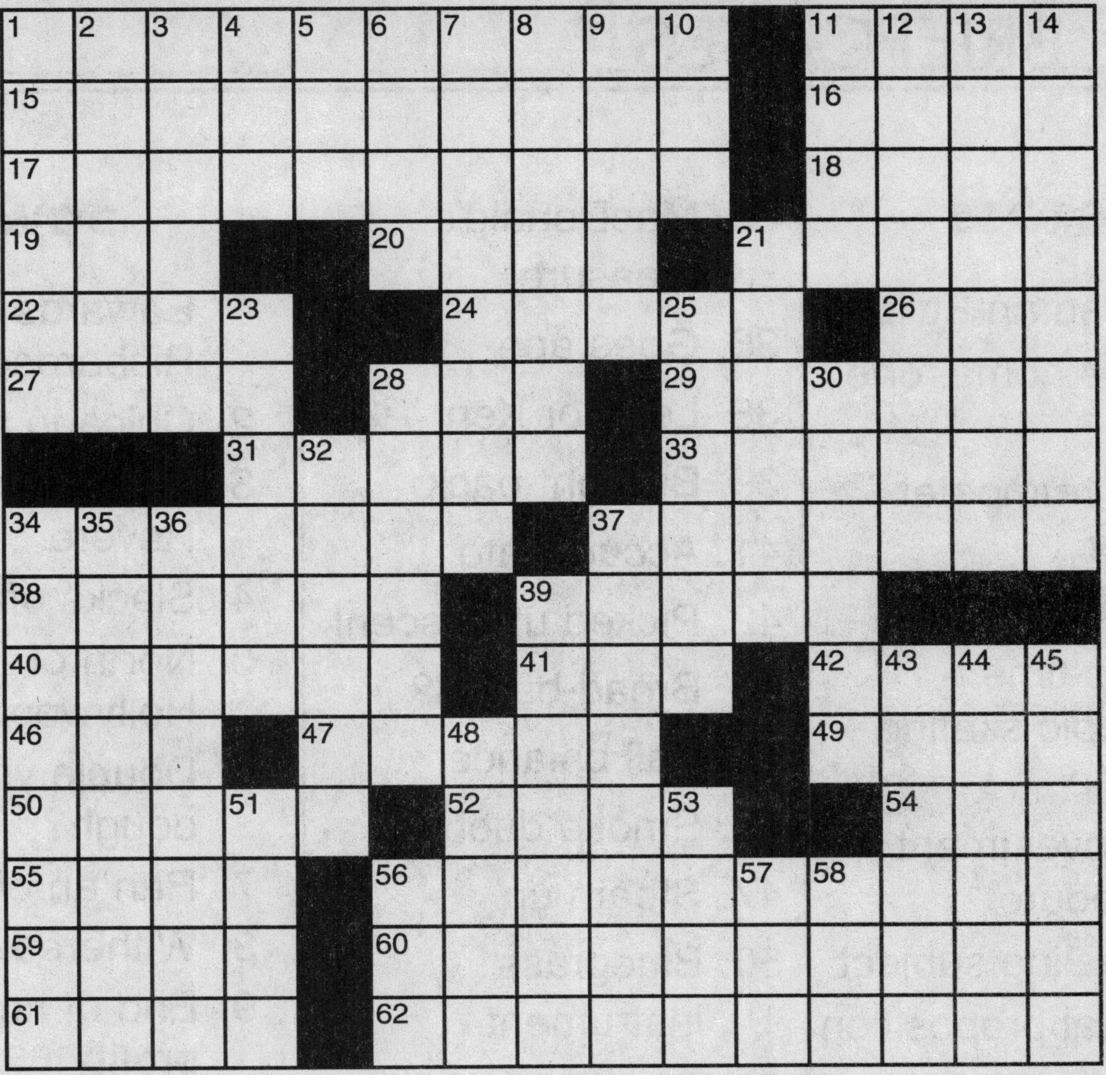

Solution is on page 223

14. American warbler

21. Fractionally

23. Portable chairs

25. Sawing wood

28. Strategic Ukrainian city

30. Quetzalcoatl's worshipers

32. Heep's namesakes

34. Vatican City sight

35. Intensified

36. Consecrate

37. It may be diplomatic

39. Imply logically

43. Detail

44. "— of Honey" (Alpert hit)

45. Fireplace facing

48. Rouen's river

51. Welfare state?

53. Scintilla

56. Except

57. Art-rocker Brian

58. *Bateau*'s domain

41 BRIEFCASES

by Robert Wolfe

ACROSS

1. Earned an Eclipse
5. Come home, one way
10. Jazz trumpeter Baker
14. Jezebel's mate
15. Three-time Olympic skating champ
16. Pre-investment procedure
17. Appealing subject
19. Biblical preposition
20. Maintained
21. Cry from the bench
22. "— So Fine" (Chiffons hit)
23. Sine qua non
24. Step on it and come in
25. Blake's night
26. Advance to the rear
30. Moleskin shade
34. Liquefy
35. MacDonald's measure
36. Goes ape
38. Lena or Ken
39. Brought back
41. Accumulate
42. Picked up a scent
43. Broad-based?
45. Ball balancer
46. Smoke duct
47. Steam up
50. Bluegrass instrument
53. Rural rest areas
55. Any of three Giants
56. Storyteller?
57. Undergo
58. Red as —
59. *Little Man* — (1991 movie)
60. Pallid
61. They're full of feet
62. Kudos from *Blood and Sand*

DOWN

1. Edwards or Richardson
2. Chicago airport
3. Midnight rider with Revere
4. Slacks off
5. North of Hollywood
6. Double your dough?
7. Ran an old press
8. Withered
9. End of racket or profit
10. Where the action is?
11. Dealer's distribution
12. Cigar stretcher
13. God of thunder
18. Comic Taylor
21. They make Trigger happy
24. Army eatery
26. Comic Taylor
27. Raines in old movies

Solution is on page 224

28. Auto renter

29. Decimal bases

30. Pastry variety

31. Service whiz

32. Major star group

33. Boxed dozen?

34. Acted

36. Loose

37. Spearheaded

40. Spread in sticks

41. Manhattan Project event

43. Imperfect

44. Return reviews

46. Home room

47. Paragon

48. Remainder, in Rouen

49. Mississippi quartet?

50. — ghanouj (eggplant dish)

51. Mugfuls at the Mermaid

52. Ancient mariner?

53. First name in Nashville

54. Sondheim's — *the Woods*

56. Actress Lenz

42 YOU SLEIGH ME

by Paul Matwychuk

ACROSS

1. Penultimate Greek letter
4. Infomercials
7. Nile nemesis
10. *Platoon* setting, for short
13. *Sturm — Drang*
14. Prefix for corn or pod
15. Cutesy suffix
16. Frankie's love
17. Goofs
19. Set dresser
21. DASHER
23. Bee's relative?
24. In the style of
25. Rat tail?
26. Part of Sydney Greenstreet's *Casablanca* costume
27. Palette choices
30. Cicatrices
31. DANCER
35. Countenance
36. Paw
37. PRANCER
42. Began at bezique
44. Goodall subjects
45. Pick
46. Break — (play sudden death)
47. Peter O'Toole's *Stunt Man* role
49. Asian nurse
50. VIXEN
55. — passage
56. Australopithecine
58. "Yahoo!" in Yucatan
59. Stretch (out)
60. Classic Steely Dan album
61. Business bigwig, briefly
62. Composer Rorem
63. Versifier's contraction
64. Craggy peak
65. Nightmarish street

DOWN

1. Bitter source
2. Nosy Parker
3. Deify
4. Literally, "indivisible"
5. Leave unexplored
6. Emphatically yes, to José
7. Overcome with horror
8. Not 'zactly
9. Wol's friend
10. Conventioneer's introduction
11. Incarnation
12. Certain impressionist masterpieces
18. Tournament pass
20. The in — be (hot spot)
22. *Hacienda*, e.g.
23. Spoilt
27. Sister's outfit

84

Solution is on page 224

28. Cynically manipulated
29. Marion or Jean ender
30. Writer Vikram and family
32. Sara's "Roseanne" role
33. Sleepyhead's protest
34. Provoke

37. Made up
38. Readily, once
39. Steel product?
40. Springer or clumber
41. Old English letter
42. Miracle synthetic
43. *Le soleil, par exemple*

47. Call out
48. Pro con?
49. Athos, to Aramis
51. "Understood!"
52. Indian mountain pass
53. Sgt. Yemana's coworker
54. *Juice* actor Epps
57. Cleric's title

PICTURE THI$

by Bob Sefick

ACROSS

1. D.C. pros
5. Guzzle
9. Search through
13. Border upon
14. Daryl's partner
15. Atom with a negative charge
17. WASHINGTONS
19. Rod in tennis
20. Overseers
21. Compulsion
22. Attorneys' charges
23. Garb for Giselle
24. Journalistic query
25. Annual climber
28. Elites' relatives
31. Patience player's concern
32. Lode stone?
33. Mind
34. Wells' partner
35. Marquee name
36. Fountain, for one
37. Icicles' locale
38. Full of talk
39. Hamburger Helper, e.g.
41. Blunderbuss
42. Importuned
43. "— phone!"
47. Parlor chair
49. Kinsman
50. Closing of parliament?
51. MCKINLEY
52. Sherlock's *femme fatale*
53. Resentment
54. Geometer's calculation
55. Former JFK sights
56. Reputation
57. Uses batting

DOWN

1. Like yesterday's fad
2. Final notices?
3. Director Sidney
4. "Love Boat" problem
5. What non-musicians play
6. Famous 41-Down
7. Bed-and-breakfasts
8. War movie extras
9. Greets formally
10. Overcome with ennui
11. LINCOLNS
12. Digits
16. Digits, briefly
18. Carpenters' lumber
21. Because of
23. Fire starters
25. More dextrous
26. Times to remember

Solution is on page 224

27. Frothy, to the Bard

28. Innocent, e.g.

29. Long-horned goat

30. FRANKLINS

31. Squirreled away

34. Covers, in craps

35. Hazard for 41-Down

37. "Gentlemen, start your —!"

38. *The — Archipelago* (Solzhenitsyn)

40. Like some knights

41. One who's teed off?

43. Surprised expression

44. Victoria's crown

45. Put an edge on

46. *— a Man* (Willingham novel)

47. A month in Paris

48. NHL's Bobby and family

49. Commando action

51. Cable listing

by Richard Thomas

ACROSS

1. Computer cousins
6. It's a real butte
10. Historic isle
14. Michener title
15. Encumbrance
16. Tale type
17. Swerves
18. Long gone
19. Talk up
20. EAST
23. Paved the way
24. Alpine region
25. Ran the meeting
29. Branch bit
33. Chilean cape
34. Caribbean resort
38. Lisbon lady
39. Where 11-Down is
40. *Two Women* star
41. Inconsequential
42. Brief gander
43. Outpouring
44. Pulitzer winner James
45. Where the elite meet
47. Fowl parts
49. In need of caulking
53. These, in Tours
54. WEST
61. Tombstone lawman
62. Cooperstown's Johnny
63. 78-card game
64. *Pinta* partner
65. Prolific auth.
66. Pay to stay
67. Job or line starter
68. Inert gas
69. — Park, CO

DOWN

1. Off-road trans.
2. Sugar source
3. Fleming feat
4. SOUTH
5. Dispenser
6. Does floors
7. Perform
8. Fish dish
9. Up and about
10. NORTH
11. Vientiane's land
12. Cerulean
13. Canadian prov.
21. Noble goals
22. Some votes
25. Cowpoke pants

Solution is on page 224

26. Hebrew prophet

27. Prospero's spirit

28. Parachute

30. — et noir (betting game)

31. Creek

32. Flag flappers

35. Neighbor of Arg.

36. Ocean hazard

37. Cutup's tricks

46. USA member

48. Bailey of the comics

50. Jordan's capital

51. Artist Franz

52. Vicksburg's river

54. Poulards

55. First felon

56. Tuscan river

57. Colonial Quaker

58. "Shucks!"

59. It takes your breath away

60. Tops tortes

by Ernie Furtado

ACROSS

1. Start of a series
4. Hip
7. Summarize briefly
12. Restrain
14. Hit it off?
15. They're all arms
16. First clue to the puzzle
19. Where ends meet
20. Third Reich chronicler's monogram
21. *Sra.*, in Seattle
22. Second names of Roman citizens
25. Do a Little bit
27. Second clue to the puzzle
33. Jason's ship
34. Barometer of econ. activity
35. Rooms of one's own
36. Seek office
37. Answer to 27-Across
38. Answer to 44-Across
39. Capone's prosecutor
40. A lot of scents
42. Cannon attachment?
43. Psychoanalyst Freud
44. Third clue to the puzzle
47. Shoe size
48. Wrapping paper
49. Start of many sequel titles
51. QB targets
52. Pique period
55. Last clue to the puzzle
61. Shaquille and Ryan
62. Mind reading?
63. Minnesota player
64. Puccini opera
65. "Zip-a-Dee-Doo-—"
66. Had a hero

DOWN

1. One in any suit
2. Brooklyn Dodgers, to fans
3. Rock group Mötley —
4. Came upon
5. Pay dirt
6. Drafted
7. Nipper's logo
8. Ordinal suffix
9. Giving a boost to
10. On — with (equal to)
11. Etui fillers
13. Spanish white
15. Choice indicators
17. A way to run
18. Rat on
23. "Holy cow!"
24. "There — Greater Love"
25. Yours, to Yvonne
26. Answer to 55-Across

Solution is on page 225

27. Siddons of the stage
28. Pass-through to Provincetown
29. Scandals
30. Grooved joints
31. Horn-shaped structure
32. Elian output
37. Rubberneck
38. Thous

41. Answer to 16-Across
42. Like Napoleon at Elba
43. Political scientist Hannah
45. Another, in Barcelona
46. Bounce
49. Ayr man
50. "Yes —?"

51. Fields and Handy
53. Hawkeye State
54. Chaff
56. Second X or O, gamewise
57. Bloc on the docks
58. Shooter ammo
59. Cry of disgust
60. Ship's dir.

46 LITERAL HITS

by D.J. DeChristopher

ACROSS

1. Asset
5. Seat for the masses
8. Santa's reindeer, e.g.
12. Fish spear
14. Spark, in a way
16. Begum's counterpart
17. Escapade
18. Stick targets
19. *Exodus* penner
20. Romantic prefix
21. Jim Croce hit, literally
24. Estuary
25. Kitchen utensil
26. Gazpacho ingredient
29. Pointillist's unit
30. Aerosmith hit, literally
36. Take a wild swing
37. Border
38. Nest eggs, for short
40. Bruce Springsteen hit, literally
45. "Fish" star Vigoda
46. Sometime in the future
47. Fleet
51. Long tales
53. Beatles hit, literally
55. Curtain call
58. "— Rose" (*The Music Man* song)
59. Reverse
60. South American ruminant
62. Premed course
63. Connery or Penn
64. Rocklike
65. Flatfish
66. WSW opposite
67. Dentist's concern

DOWN

1. Blueprint
2. Highway path
3. "For — us a child is born…"
4. —-fi (genre for 15-Down)
5. Airborne driver
6. Lily persona
7. Blubbered
8. Aligns properly
9. Terra firma
10. Doddering
11. Cheapskate to the max
13. 32-card game
15. Prolific Isaac
22. See 62-Across
23. First name in spydom

Solution is on page 225

24. Deceitful
26. Scotsman's topper
27. Step — (rush)
28. Netting
29. Bruce's ex
31. French river
32. Actor Morrow
33. Ocean motion
34. Toward the mouth

35. — avis
39. Ether
41. Arp's movement
42. Early counter
43. Yuletide drinks
44. Growls
47. Book of maps
48. Tropical herbivore
49. Olympic prize

50. Lessen
51. African land
52. United
54. Kind of jerk?
55. Java neighbor
56. Neglect
57. Wimbledon champ of '77
61. Stroke for 57-Down

by Paul Cutajar

ACROSS

1. Actor Culkin, to pals
4. Loud sound
7. Not, in Nantes
10. Biff's brother, briefly
13. Feel unwell
14. John of Liverpool
15. Make a request
16. Midwest tribe
17. I
19. Helmsman
21. X
23. Composer Reynaldo
25. Dinghy thingy
26. How one has to be in France?
27. "You — So Beautiful"
28. Moslem call to prayer
31. Less sweet, winewise
32. M
36. Golfer's conveyance
37. Actress Skye
38. V
43. Yoga position
45. Former Angel pitcher Don
46. "Mister Basketball" Holman
47. City on the Oka
48. NBC weekend fare
50. Seventies hairstyle
51. C
56. Frank who played the Riddler
57. Oilers' province
60. Inventor Whitney
61. Chemical suffix
62. Preceder of *tre*
63. Roman goddess of night
64. Room for the kids
65. "The Strife Is —" (Christian hymn)
66. Aquatic shocker
67. One of Pooh's pals

DOWN

1. Glove compartment item
2. Word before bag or brush
3. Covered, as in snow
4. International coalition
5. Month of *été*
6. — *Lisa*
7. Elbows on the table?
8. Fur trader John Jacob
9. —-Ball (arcade game)
10. Hamlet addressee
11. Ballet phrase meaning "on the ground"
12. A real pig
18. See 28-Down
20. She comes out
22. Electricity: abbr.
23. Japheth's brother
24. Curve

Solution is on page 225

28. With 18-Down, noted diarist
29. Cup holder
30. Meter lead-in
31. Charity recipient
33. Blocks out, as a star
34. "The Destroyer"
35. Cause for elimination
38. Waxy fatty acid

39. It's #1 on Mohs' scale
40. Part of the *Divine Comedy*
41. Sense organ
42. *Pou* — (base of operations)
43. He's been taken in
44. Cal Ripkin Jr., e.g.
48. Maliciously superior

49. Candlestick gridder, for short
50. Hops to it?
52. Where to find Columbus
53. "Smooth Operator" singer
54. This is one
55. Director Ferrara
58. AAA offering
59. Rock's Rose

by Joel Hess

ACROSS

1. Nonecclesiastical
5. Songwriters' org.
10. Dog in Camp Swampy
14. River of Catalonia
15. ——-*feuille* (flaky pastry)
16. It follows function
17. Novelist Paton
18. She got advice from a caterpillar
19. Col. Mustard's game
20. Why Pinocchio makes such a dreadful actor
23. Storm center
24. Hokkaido native
25. It's a bumbershoot in Bristol
30. Saint from Ávila
34. Comedian Louis
35. Ugly, in Orly
37. Flower symbol of September
38. Why Porky Pig makes such a dreadful actor
42. Start of a Desilu Productions title
43. Either of the stars of *Tea and Sympathy*
44. Stout relative
45. Part of A.D.
47. Intensified
50. Vapor: prefix
52. Bern's river
53. Why the fisherman makes such a dreadful actor
61. Cultural beginning
62. Bikini blast
63. — voce (orally)
64. NEWS announcer?
65. Cotton thread
66. Highest pair
67. Deputy Sheriff Strate
68. Loosened up
69. Hawaii's state bird

DOWN

1. Laban's elder daughter
2. Strong enough
3. She dies with Cleo
4. Meet
5. Variety of cherry
6. River sediment
7. Euterpe's sister
8. Pittsburgh corporation
9. Onomatopoetic bird
10. "Naturally"
11. Squealed
12. "I see your point"
13. Foretoken
21. Senatorial assent
22. Streisand's *The Main Event* costar
25. In plain sight, poetically
26. Marrow: prefix
27. Twig broom

Solution is on page 225

28. Member of an exaltation
29. Broadcast
31. Filmmaker Joel Coen's brother
32. '60s radical Bobby
33. Ready to do battle
36. Voir —
39. They're for the birds

40. —-one odds
41. Braved the waves
46. Stick with a stake
48. Joey, for one
49. Capital of Armenia
51. Port of ancient Rome
53. Eat or drink
54. "Magnet and Steel" singer

55. Bond flick set in Jamaica
56. Medicine Nobelist Walter
57. Avalon, for one
58. Capital of Alpes-Maritimes
59. Divisible by two
60. Mail offer respondent's encl.

by Norman Wizer

ACROSS

1. Fissure
5. Turnpike take
9. Harvard section
13. City in Kansas
14. Actress O'Donnell
15. Man or Wight
16. Most animals?
18. Surrender
19. Is, to Cicero
20. Albatross
21. Hindu maxims
23. Summon
24. Computer listing
25. City on the Loire
27. Voiced consonant
31. Larry of "Hogan's Heroes"
32. Ceremony
33. Lamb pseudonym
34. Acting Idle
35. Stupefied
36. Derive
37. Descend gradually
38. Arden and Plumb
39. Quickly
40. Ingredients in lacquers
42. Accustom
43. Harrow rival
44. Sea eagle
45. Flower part
48. She runs the *Haus*
49. Piece by Pindar
52. Half of *dix*
53. Engaged in a water sport?
56. Comic Johnson
57. Trunks
58. Maple leaf or tricolor
59. Rathskeller offering
60. Perry's creator
61. Tim Daly's sib

DOWN

1. Mature
2. Chits
3. *Pied-à-terre*
4. Little bit
5. Chef's hat
6. Sugary endings
7. Pot top
8. Eased off
9. Scenic?
10. Employer
11. *Manhattan Murder Mystery* star
12. Sub-par grades
14. Crosspieces
17. MGM opening sounds
22. Article in *La Prensa*?
23. Short fuse?

Solution is on page 226

24. Dust specks

25. Donut-shaped

26. Like Aries

27. Dimensions

28. Place for 32-Across

29. Dorothy, to Em

30. Submissive

31. "For — jolly…"

32. Poetic bird

35. Set off

39. Cancel

41. Consumed

42. Arbil native

44. Clean the slate

45. Picket-line crosser

46. Bore

47. Pay to play

48. Roll up a sail

49. "— the Lonely"

50. College VIP

51. Advantage

54. "— favor, Señor"

55. Educators' org.

CONSUMMATE CONSONANTS

by Harvey Estes

ACROSS

1. Working parents' recourse
8. Gen. Arnold
11. Douglas is one
14. Shipfitter
15. Brabantio's son-in-law
17. Open-door policy?
18. Masked skaters
19. Beatles' record company
20. Movie studio's Fords
21. Slant
23. Employ the eyes
24. Salmon or peach
27. And the like: abbr.
29. Near
33. Political refugees, often
36. Egypt and Syr., once
39. Opinion
40. Government support
41. Solicits
43. Past
44. Teacher's favorite
45. Funny law?
46. Horne of plenty of music
48. Judge Fortas
50. Dick Tracy's girl
51. — Paulo
54. Rapture
57. Presidential briefs
61. Louganis, for one
64. Some protozoans
65. Ballot brandisher
67. Radio cabinet
68. What de teacher gives?
69. Shortened heart test
70. 5 ml.
71. Plaited

DOWN

1. Lawn wetter
2. Perimeter insides
3. Screech
4. Red spy group, once
5. Strand of land
6. Tragic lover
7. Before of yore
8. Hazzard's Boss
9. Molecule members
10. Aspect
11. Fly flippantly
12. "— Three Lives"
13. Patriotic seamstress
16. Actress Burstyn
20. He'll play at Shea
22. Barcelona bread
24. Flower fragment
25. It's made of pixels
26. Haldeman's boss

Solution is on page 226

28. Compact club

30. Children

31. Frenchmen

32. Promotes showily

34. Bum follower

35. Compass pt.

37. Constellation near Pavo

38. Toupee

42. "The A-Team" star's tape players

47. Fools

49. Air rifle output

52. Monastery manager

53. Racetracks

55. Goldbrick

56. Military blockade

57. Arsenic's old companion

58. U. hotshot

59. Author Erica

60. Well-hidden

62. H H H

63. Avoided walking

65. Watch-changing letters

66. Buttons on the TV

51 WOK NEXT?

by Raymond Hamel

ACROSS

1. Harriet, to Dick Grayson
5. 1965 Andress film
8. Sail-extending spar
13. Kind of code
15. Tex-— cuisine
16. Instruct
17. Ferrule for a cord
18. Ballpark figure
19. Total
20. America, metaphorically
23. Ossian's land
24. Plod
25. A sweetener
27. Marjorie Main role
31. Area between outfielders
32. Dos Passos trilogy
33. Cover a falcon's eyes
34. Variety of clam
38. "The Swedish Nightingale"
40. Intent
43. Literary captain
44. Respond to avidly
46. Old Anglo-Saxon coins
48. Lagniappe
49. Wall St. watchdog
51. Die cutter's pattern
53. Popular snack
57. Foil alternative
58. Dagwood's neighbor
59. Bizarre
64. Homer king
66. Chaotic place
67. Richard of *Guadalcanal Diary*
68. Author of *Oldtown Folks*
69. Stop — dime
70. Bergen's dummy Klinker
71. Jubal of the Confederacy
72. Beatty of "Homicide"
73. Former Senator from Kentucky

DOWN

1. Sistine ceiling figure
2. Advocate strongly
3. Jodie Foster role
4. Dreaded fly
5. Fly-by-night operator
6. Fiber of 37-Down
7. Washington Nationals, before
8. Basketball coach Jackson
9. Shadow seeker of fiction
10. 7:1, e.g.
11. Cupcake frosters
12. Dimensional starter
14. Leg extenders
21. Famous
22. McGraw of diamond fame
26. Game show giveaway
27. Slipper

Solution is on page 226

28. Prometheus' wife, according to Shelley
29. German philosopher (1724-1804)
30. Mary Ann Evans' alias
35. Greek letter
36. Leave out
37. Strong cord

39. 1930s drought region
41. Sponge
42. Florida sports town
45. Candy in a dispenser
47. British pantry
50. Corp. bigwig
52. Batted first
53. Aspect

54. Lasso
55. Breach of judgment
56. Manila's island
60. Shade
61. Data
62. Pokey
63. Pay attention
65. Napoleon's marshal

52 ANCIENT CONCLAVE

by Arthur S. Verdesca

ACROSS

1. Carlsbad Caverns denizens
5. Gropes
10. Throw slowly in an arc
13. It's a lot to live on
14. Where wheels spin
15. Facility
16. Start of an old news bulletin
19. Hesitate in speaking
20. "Behold, Brutus!"
21. The end
22. Macaulay Culkin persona, often
23. Varanasi, once
25. Thorough
28. Vampire weapons
29. Weed whacker
30. Spotted
31. Huckster's output
34. Middle of the bulletin
38. Perennial plot?
39. Camel lots
40. BBs
41. Welcome word
42. Most inadequate
44. Ramble
47. Karma
48. Pass over
49. Off the wall
50. Cannon attachment?
53. End of the bulletin
57. Aldebaran, e.g.
58. Resident of Latium
59. She played Lois
60. Still
61. Stone marker
62. Really impressed

DOWN

1. First of the three B's
2. Long
3. Defeat
4. Get it
5. Garfield?
6. Force payment of
7. First name of 1902 and 1986 Peace Nobelists
8. Actor Cariou
9. Draft org.
10. Carpet installer
11. Largest tributary of the Missouri
12. Constellations' second-brightest stars
15. Bombeck namesakes
17. Spore producer
18. Black tea from China
22. Cutting remark
23. Judges' seats
24. Within: prefix
25. Melville's hunter
26. Ceremonial dress
27. Perceive in print
28. Traffic court judge, often

Solution is on page 226

30. Baffling question
31. Peak
32. Lowers the headlights
33. Coin collector
35. Over there
36. Like the White Rabbit
37. Specify
41. Swimmer Kornelia
42. Hiatus
43. Scintilla
44. Embarrassing
45. Remove by dissolving
46. Target
47. Word with plane or point
49. Rickey ingredient
50. Once more
51. Terrible
52. Markey who played Tarzan's Jane
54. Part of the Treasury Dept.
55. W.C. Fields portrayal
56. Airport abbr.

SINGLE-MINDEDNESS

by Harvey Estes

ACROSS

1. Egyptian biter
4. Spoken
8. Solder relative
14. Where a *bateau* sails
15. God forerunner?
16. Where catchers work
17. Bargain hunter's break
19. Noted bridge expert
20. Buchwald or Barry
21. Shankar strums some
22. Minaret man
23. Modem connector: abbr.
24. Lt. maker
25. Verb of poverty
27. See 14-Across
29. Strong longings
33. *République du —* (African country, officially)
35. Brace for the cold
37. Baloney
38. Kind
39. Flushed
40. Coconut-orange dessert
42. Short and sweet
43. — majesty
44. Photo
45. Indicates thumbs up
46. Thole pole
48. King Arthur's foster brother
50. Rick Nelson's "Teen Age —"
54. A rival of Arantxa
57. Popular competition
59. Author of *The Compleat Angler*
60. Put in a particular position
61. "Pogo" alligator
62. Preminger of premieres
63. I, Claudius?
64. King Kong killers
65. Madeline of *Blazing Saddles*
66. Tribe of Israel

DOWN

1. Theater front?
2. Vehicle for antibodies
3. "Just a Gigolo" Louis
4. Baltic feeder
5. Declaimed
6. Tell jokes, for example
7. SINGLE FILE
8. Distribute or drop
9. Moral standard
10. SINGLE OPENING
11. 1/3 of a war movie
12. Kuwaiti chieftain
13. Men with yellow flags

Solution is on page 227

18. SINGLE LINE

26. Best in boxing

28. Northern fowl

30. They seldom meet

31. Painting type

32. Bond, for one

33. Volume

34. Kernel holders

36. Take a tough trip

37. *2001* computer

38. King George's train?

41. Runs lickety-split

42. Tease

47. Mentioned earlier?

49. Heart connection

51. Passé

52. Symbol of resistance

53. Taken down the primrose path

54. Trade

55. Having high standing?

56. Exile isle

58. Jaworski of Watergate

by Norma Steinberg

ACROSS

1. What you used to be
5. Imperturbable
9. Place for a pin
12. Astronomer Carl
14. Topping for a stack
15. He wrote about Rosemary
16. OTO
18. Cacophony
19. Nit-picker
20. Mont. neighbor
21. Palm an ace, perhaps
24. It's grainy
26. Gladden
28. Susanna's accusers
31. Catch aurally
32. Describe a hit
35. Tenant before Jackie

36. Sale tag abbr.
37. Announces
39. Call for Maria
40. —-frutti
42. Low joint?
43. Wheels for wee ones, at Windsor
44. On the train
46. Means of expression
48. — a bird
51. Trails
52. Deep sleepers?
54. Mass activity
56. Past
57. TAG
62. Not normal
63. Teamsters, e.g.
64. Bart's dad
65. Make hay while the sun shines
66. First place
67. Life partner

DOWN

1. Child's meas.
2. "Gotcha!"
3. Shrink's scrutiny
4. Down a sub
5. Doubter
6. Go up
7. Patina, in Perth
8. Dashboard info
9. ARC
10. Notes from Domingo
11. Aquarium
13. Bond description
14. Peter Ustinov's title
17. It's sure to make history
20. Zilch
21. Baby angel
22. OL
23. Racket attachment?

Solution is on page 227

25. *Desire Under the —*

26. Dancer Rivera

27. Stow the Chevy

29. Contenders

30. Plea from The Who's Tommy

33. Halen or Heflin

34. Hgt.

37. Put on staff

38. More profound

41. Sailors

43. Avocado stone

45. Rely

47. Severe

49. Palmer with an army

50. Squelched

52. *Café* lightener

53. Have a fresh look?

55. Compulsion

57. Feed an old line to

58. Landry or Bosley

59. PAC of physicians

60. Obtain

61. Two-way preposition

by Jon Delfin

ACROSS

1. Shields or Yarnell
5. Pier
10. Missing in inaction?
14. "Now — me down…"
15. "— Yo" (Ruth B. Hill saga)
16. Composer Harold
17. What this answer isn't
20. Start of a Fitzgerald title
21. Doctoral requirement, often
22. Gore, before: abbr.
23. Pass up
24. Takes on
28. Jot
29. Hen's mate
32. Photo tint
33. Iranian title
34. It's hereditary
35. How this answer isn't
38. Writer Bontemps
39. Allot (with "out")
40. Showing celerity
41. Actress Carrie
42. Fit
43. Gets serious (with "up")
44. Skip
45. Snit
46. Cheap
49. Referees
54. Where this answer isn't
56. Son of Zeus
57. Legislate
58. Sacrifice
59. Director Clair
60. U.S. Grant's foe
61. "Snake eyes"

DOWN

1. New, as a coin
2. "Nasty" tennis pro
3. School reformer Horace
4. Gave a once-over to
5. — *Charley?*
6. With — hand (humbly)
7. Farm insects
8. Hwy.
9. 1/4 penny, once
10. Composer Harold
11. Courts
12. Old Atlanta arena
13. Hypotenuse neighbors
18. *The Vampire* — (Anne Rice novel)
19. Close
23. 1953 Ladd film
24. Egyptian dam
25. Northern Ireland county
26. Conjecture
27. Sandwich pocket

Solution is on page 227

28. *Charlotte's Web* writer

29. Arizona State's city

30. How the elated walk

31. Repairs

33. Faced a queen?

34. Impress

36. Make resentful

37. Suggestive, in a way

42. Infamous Ugandan

43. Composed

44. Beyond plump

45. At least eight 9-Downs

46. Mogul

47. Used to be

48. Chamber for curing

49. Farina

50. With the bow

51. Roger Rabbit, for one

52. Being: Lat.

53. Mach 2 travelers

55. 67 1/2°, on the compass

by Alex Vaughn

ACROSS

1. Trump's strong suit?
6. Mt. Rushmore state
10. Phi Bete's report card?
14. Circuit for Saturn
15. Leander's love
16. V-J Day ended it
17. Piratic Punjabi prince
19. Take shape
20. Sugar suffix
21. — monster
22. Reproductive bodies
24. Clue
25. Bipartite
26. Jane Darwell, in *The Grapes of Wrath*
29. — the Bulge
33. — *Like Alice* (1956 film)
34. Author Garborg
35. One of the Ivies
36. Milk or chamber follower
37. Roaring twenties pocketful
38. British carbine
39. Mrs. Charles Laughton
40. Sow sound
41. Stampede stimulus
42. On a leash
44. Seat of power
45. Signify sleepiness
46. Last name in espionage
47. Goddess of the dawn
50. Desiccated
51. Ripen
54. Bremen brew
55. Punjabi cold symptoms
58. Troop
59. Dew unit
60. Blithering one
61. With 49-Down, losers
62. Makes clothes
63. Merry Man Allan

DOWN

1. Karate studio
2. Cupid
3. Competent
4. Diamond lady?
5. Murky and malefic
6. Commandment verb
7. — *vu*
8. Coach Parseghian
9. 1973 comet
10. Punjabi apology
11. He's way off base
12. Leeds river
13. Lines up cross hairs
18. Fruit cover
23. Dye tub
24. Punjabi mahout's greeting
25. Danish, in Danish

Solution is on page 227

26. *Speed-the-Plow* playwright David
27. "And thereby hangs —" (Shakespeare)
28. Floor-support beam
29. Cattle marking
30. "...could — fat"
31. Liquid fraction of fat
32. He handles hot stuff
34. Green-card carrier
37. Sends a letter on
41. Mind: suffix
43. Dumbo's "wing"
44. Biblical weed
46. Uriah and his mum
47. Rhyme scheme
48. Russian river
49. See 61-Across
50. Winter fall
51. Most people live there
52. Earth sci.
53. Italy's Villa d'—
56. Is plural
57. Singular

by David Rosen

ACROSS

1. Ling and burbot
5. Pole, for example
9. Islamic holy war
14. Cartel begun 9/14/60
15. Singer's rival
16. — *Time* (Broadway musical)
17. Goya subject
18. Cat's-paw
19. Hindu habit
20. Instructions to make this entry fit
23. Populous place
24. Burns and Allen's announcer Harry Von —
25. Legrand of movie music
28. Put the arm on
32. "A hairy quadruped, furnished with —" (Darwin)
33. Unit of magnetic induction
34. Thai tongue
35. DEA gumshoe
36. Neighbor of Nîmes
37. Shipboard petty officer
38. Approval for a veronica
39. Butterfingers
40. Parceled (out)
41. Up — (anybody's, potentially)
43. Prince Charles' first wife
44. Canine health-food brand
45. Number of Dionne *enfants*
46. Instructions to make this entry fit
53. Hashemi Rafsanjani, e.g.
54. Bee or Em
55. *"Dies —"* (requiem hymn)
56. First Clown, in *Pagliacci*
57. Forged check
58. Retreat
59. Of yore
60. School founded by Henry VI
61. Pericles' princedom

DOWN

1. Search meticulously
2. Milky stone
3. — *vu*
4. Pertaining to chess
5. Tevye's Anatevka, for one
6. Crackers
7. Guardhouse candidate
8. Painter Diego
9. Shoves roughly
10. Facilitate
11. Stretched-out sandwich
12. NYC bourse
13. Female deer
21. Canal to the North Sea

Solution is on page 228

22. Ted Geisel's pseudonym
25. — *La Mancha*
26. Fantasist Calvino
27. Concerned party
28. Cures
29. 100 groszy
30. Moved slowly
31. Comic-strip adoptee

33. Venture capital
36. Mission to remember
37. Patchwork cover
39. Bivouac chow
40. *Hacienda* hand
42. — Mae (mortgage financer)
43. Enjoy the music

45. Patchwork poem
46. Half a Cugat hit
47. River to the Caspian
48. Howard Roark's creator
49. Almost *neuf*
50. Cigarette holder
51. Locks
52. See 46-Across

by William Lutwiniak

ACROSS

1. "…goes out like —"
6. Bowed
11. "— out of your mind?!"
12. Soaps star Hall
14. Gem of a playwright?
17. "Did gyre and gimble in the —" (Carroll)
18. Perry of fashion
19. Johnny Reb's govt.
20. Roster of preferred people
22. -trix
23. Cries for veronicas
24. Brewed leaves
25. Section of pix
27. Staffordshire river
28. Ohio family of statesmen
29. Threaten
30. Gem of a jazz pianist?
34. Hosts
35. Lotharios
36. Corresponded
37. Suit to —
38. Raconteur, often
41. Father of modern surgery
42. Tennis units
44. Beam
46. Alma-—, Kazakhstan
47. High, to Henri
49. Brilliance
50. Gem of a political columnist?
54. *2001…* writer
55. With finesse
56. No alternatives
57. Stall

DOWN

1. Asian peninsula
2. Laws: Lat.
3. Thumbs-up vote
4. Style
5. Italian burlesque of yore
6. Let in or let on
7. Brooklyn shortstop of yore
8. Townie
9. Old English letter
10. Use naphtha on
11. Start of a Dickens title
13. Fundamental part
14. Hostage-dealing team
15. Dense gray cloud
16. Tries some
21. Kerry's county seat
23. Birds of a region

Solution is on page 228

26. Eliminates, gangland-style

27. Snickers

28. Timeworn

29. Earn

30. Tree of the South

31. On-again, off-again

32. Without principle

33. Foyer feature, maybe

38. In a crafty way

39. Winglike

40. Littler or Wilder

42. Gesture of agreement

43. Contour-chair designer

45. Maestro Zubin

48. Something to fence with

51. Strategic town of New Guinea

52. Report your nanny to them

53. Chum

by Jean Davison

ACROSS

1. Attacks a fly
6. Take it easy
10. Wee
14. King of the airwaves
15. City in Yemen
16. *Dies* —
17. Making molehills out of mountains
19. Tad
20. Harper Valley org.
21. Cinematic pig
22. Depict
24. Constituents of salts
25. Lacks what it takes
26. Character in *A Chorus Line*
29. Hardest thing about riding a bicycle?
33. Moves to the runway
34. Edith Evans' title
35. Rent-— agency
36. Spot of wine
37. Started a crop
38. Carryall
39. — *Yesterday*
40. Singer Laine
41. Hardware supply
42. Took on the fly
44. Darlings
45. Tarzan's foster family
46. Sounds from the cote
47. Shakespearean weaver
50. Gossett and Gehrig
51. Palm Springs, e.g.
54. Butter rival
55. Annoyance
58. Blueprint
59. Cozy corner
60. Correct a thesis
61. Donaldson and Kinison
62. Magazine articles?
63. Swell

DOWN

1. Freudian garment?
2. Cool one's heels
3. *Aïda* highlight
4. Angle opener
5. Keyboard's top row, in shift
6. Flock members
7. Woodworking tool
8. Buddhist sect
9. Like some invitations
10. Subtle hints
11. Walked all over
12. Fill to the rim
13. Wine connoisseur's statistic
18. Darling dog
23. Compass point
24. Fraternity rites

Solution is on page 228

25. Small role

26. Wild tries

27. Wears

28. Supernumerary

29. Handled clumsily

30. Place for *un maître*

31. Cooper's Bumppo

32. Lock

34. Influential D.C. couple

37. Crafty

41. Increased

43. USN rank comparable to sgt. first class

44. Class period, often

46. Stoppers

47. Conks

48. Spicy stew

49. Paired horses

50. Symbol of Haile Selassie

51. British firearm

52. Fishing hole

53. Opie's pa

56. Debtor's letters

57. Surgeon's gp.

by Richard Silvestri

ACROSS

1. Attacks
6. Lucky guy?
11. Something to pass
14. "Dallas" matriarch
15. *My Cousin Vinny* actress
16. Plastic — Band
17. Writer's prison?
19. First-aid case
20. Kind of ring
21. Fashion designer Simpson
23. 1/10,000,000 joule
24. Put on ice
26. Skid row relative
30. Abates
31. Ken and Lena
32. Ring around the castle
33. Vincent Lopez theme
36. Washday residue
37. Birdie beater
38. WBA outcomes
39. Person of action
40. Mob scene
41. City on the Aire
42. Picks at
44. —-waiting (royal attendant)
45. Science of sound
47. — Gardens, London
48. Plunders
49. To a certain degree
54. Wright wing
55. Recycler's jail?
58. Pub potable
59. Hypnotic looks
60. Adult insect
61. Neighbor of Leb.
62. Sister of Osbert and Sacheverell
63. Whitehall whitewalls

DOWN

1. Weigh by lifting
2. Shampoo ingredient
3. Pivot
4. "— That a Shame"
5. Leashes
6. He was a Police man
7. Chinese secret society
8. Little devil
9. It's charged
10. Tournament decider
11. Dancers' lockup?
12. Old-womanish
13. Lugged
18. Spacious
22. Unnerved
24. Coped

Solution is on page 228

25. Kitchen extension

26. Forward

27. Mixed bag

28. Yuppies' clink?

29. Contest hopeful

30. Corporate emblems

32. Posts

34. Lombardy town

35. Pt. of AHA

37. Idle fellow

41. Matter for a civil court

43. Countenance

44. Pastrami preference

45. Entreaties

46. Maté source

47. Deli buy

49. "Since — You Baby"

50. Tube trophy

51. Cape Fear's st.

52. Stuffing spice

53. Cain's nephew

56. Stripling

57. Israeli weapon

by Len Elliott

ACROSS

1. Football maker
5. Leg bones
10. Still under the covers
14. Butter sub
15. Fateful card?
16. Fashioned
17. Bridge expert Sharif
18. — of Two Cities
19. A snap
20. She married Irving Thalberg
23. Expression of disgust
24. Is
28. Greenland settlement
31. Toy seller — Schwarz
34. "…find — for the common cold"
35. Gossipmonger Barrett
36. Batman's abode
38. Jr. college degrees
39. Occupations
40. Math operation: abbr.
41. Type of wrestling
43. What to sip in Sapporo
44. Deplete
45. Class for immigrants: abbr.
46. In or bed follower
47. Nissan model
49. In favor of
50. Mexican silents star
57. Tiny circus performer
60. Spirit in The Tempest
61. Reasons for overtimes
62. Take five
63. Full
64. Beehive State
65. Chip in
66. Toboggans
67. Vicki Lawrence role

DOWN

1. Hands up time
2. Sailors' saint
3. Kind of admiral
4. A = L x W, e.g.
5. Hidden stuff
6. "What — God wrought!"
7. "Dies —"
8. Vincent Lopez's theme song
9. Metric area measure
10. Part of USA
11. Ewe said it
12. McMahon and Wynn
13. Former Tunisian title
21. Number on a cake
22. Finals
25. Ice cream treat
26. Soviet rule by three
27. Was in the military
28. Outer ear part

Solution is on page 229

29. Husky-voiced

30. Latent

31. Danish islands

32. Mornings, spelled out

33. Former Magic center

36. Kid's card game

37. Sea eagle

39. Dried coconut meat

42. Cheaply priced

43. Layer of rock

46. Pt. of USSR

48. Pile up

49. Gets out of the game

51. Spoken

52. "Nick at —"

53. Require

54. Actress Hayworth

55. Quire group

56. Fed. workplace watchdog

57. Italian monk's title

58. Baseball's Dykstra

59. Founded: abbr.

by Randy Sowell

ACROSS

1. Seward Peninsula city
5. "It's —-see show!" (critic's rave)
10. Info to input
14. Pt. of a monogram
15. Pasta cooked al —
16. Israeli statesman
17. Close
18. People of Peru
19. Irishman or Welshman
20. "On Liberty" author
23. Caper
24. Buying binges
25. Rodrigo Díaz de Bivar
27. Club for 33-Down
31. It heads south?
34. Throw out
38. French flower
39. Medieval dynasty
43. Picayune objection
44. He framed Desdemona
45. Collection
46. Nocturnal carnivores
48. Worldwide commerce grp.
51. Unicellular organism
55. Waiter's write-up
59. Sense of smell conduit
62. Miscellany
63. Objet d'art
64. Enter
65. Carolina cape
66. Garden gadget
67. — *Upon a Mattress*
68. Warning from 33-Down
69. Dodger Hall of Famer
70. Jersey cagers

DOWN

1. Oriental assassin
2. Bermuda, e.g.
3. Power
4. Like many enclaves
5. Mine entrance
6. Headwaiter's supply
7. Take the lid off
8. Brenda of the comics
9. Gave exams to
10. Judgment
11. Director Ferrara
12. Like the Sears Tower
13. Picnic visitor
21. —-fi
22. Haggard of C&W
26. Quaid/Ryan film of 1988
28. Is in contention
29. Art deco designer
30. Part of R&R

Solution is on page 229

31. Make an indelible impression
32. Open carriage
33. Golfer Ballesteros
35. One: prefix
36. RR stop
37. Children's game
40. Apronlike garment
41. South American ruminant

42. "…grace of God, —"
47. World Cup sport
49. Heavy weight
50. Trail Blazers' state
52. Piano practice piece
53. Comic musician Victor

54. First sign of spring
56. Apiary inhabitant
57. Throw out
58. Clair and Coty
59. Bread spread
60. Fibber
61. The distant past
62. Not at work

by Alex Vaughn

ACROSS

1. Rift
7. Weekly cry
11. Skater Babilonia
14. "Under —" (*The Little Mermaid* song)
15. Ring of Israelis?
16. Mouse announcement
17. Northern Ireland
18. Cohan's egg song?
20. Berlin's Halloween ballad?
22. Nickname in pinupdom
23. Part of a yen
24. St. Louis-to-Chicago dir.
25. Long-faced
28. Moravian, for one
30. *True Lies* director James
31. First name in cosmetics
34. Mullah's milieu
36. Its business is booming
37. Comedian Bert and family
38. "— the ramparts…"
39. Menachem's vis-à-vis
41. Greenpeace prefix
42. A certain *je ne sais* —
43. Scenario
44. Infatuations
47. Insipid
49. Gone — (deteriorated)
50. Tic-tac-toe win
51. Colonized critter
54. Bad-news headline
55. Jolson's Muslim melody?
58. Ellington's Greek song?
62. "Is that a fact?"
63. Staten, e.g.: abbr.
64. What the three monkeys ignore
65. Sleeping potion
66. Toothpaste choice
67. Philosophy 101 first name
68. Domestic maven

DOWN

1. Brings a toe woe
2. Elton John song
3. "— another line; can you hold?"
4. Experts' endings?
5. Grail verb
6. Lot for yachts
7. Yon things
8. Whitman of NJ, once
9. Author Levin
10. Get to the bottom of
11. Youmans' golf-date ditty?
12. Gaseous prefix
13. Dick was his veep
19. Roll response
21. Green-eyed
25. Douglas' isle

Solution is on page 229

26. Sub's pinger
27. Contest mail-in
28. Sun. oration
29. Article in *Le Monde*
30. Reindeer relative
31. Give a majority to
32. Pelvic prefix
33. Rodgers & Hart's piggery piece?

35. Old Olds
39. Simile words
40. Advanced degree?
42. Proof letters
45. Playwright O'Casey
46. Cattleman
48. *The Sea Wolf* writer
50. "— *Mio*"

51. "My heart skipped —"
52. Nick of flicks
53. Tippecanoe's pard
56. Gary Cooperism
57. "— a far, far better…"
58. Jet fighter plane
59. Exploit
60. "— been had!"
61. Card player's cry

64   MIXED-UP PEOPLE

by Matt Gaffney

ACROSS

1. Millard Fillmore was one
5. Figure who's red in the face
10. Strikebreaker
14. — Krishna
15. Steer stopper
16. Nadia's medal-winning predecessor
17. Goofy singer Lennox?
19. Old autos
20. Old West chronicler
21. Excessive affection
23. Playmate
24. Ready to buy
26. Asian structures
30. Warning sign
33. Zaragoza's river
34. Demagogue's oration
36. Porter, in a pub
37. Where seconds count
39. Welcome item
40. Committed a grammatical no-no
42. Simile center
43. Steakhouse orders
46. Rapper/actor
47. Plea from someone locked out
49. Ramble
51. Sacred river of India
53. Despicable
54. Rebel against
56. One of a nursery rhyme trio
61. They often bring change
62. High-flying former Trump?
64. Jackson 5 member
65. Overexcited
66. Skater Heiden
67. Saxophonist Getz
68. — nous
69. Nigerian-born singer

DOWN

1. Genius
2. Colleague of Steffi and Arantxa
3. Where Qum people live
4. It determines our traits
5. Try to intimidate
6. Top-notch
7. Annual Broadway celebration
8. — Lay Dying (Faulkner)
9. Ribbed
10. In a way
11. Incorruptible Judge Ito?
12. Eagerly awaiting
13. See 53-Across
18. "Zounds!"

Solution is on page 229

22. Less familiar
25. Took the stump
26. Bit of equipment for Greg LeMond
27. Coarse language
28. Terrific screen star Garbo?
29. Writer de Beauvoir
31. Soothing plants

32. Pickwick Club members
35. Quarterbacked
38. Letter taker
41. They're leased by the government
44. Star's draw
45. Golden intangible
48. Hero of Cronin's *The Citadel*
50. Asian desert

52. It can be brief
54. Young folks
55. Military group
57. Delilah's target
58. Arctic sea
59. Geraint's wife
60. Steeplechase, e.g.
63. Part of many Dutch surnames

by Morris Alpern

ACROSS

1. They have speed limits
6. Warm, fuzzy feeling
10. Painful memory
14. Baby discomfort
15. Molten rock
16. Corner of a diamond?
17. Gladiator's arena
19. Author Ludwig
20. Spark catcher
21. Olive oil jar
22. Annual shot
24. Soft as down
25. It takes a lot of heat
26. Title some deplore
27. Snow remover
28. Pass by
30. Algonquian language
33. Golden-haired Lee of song
34. Actor Vigoda
35. Shankar specialty
37. Like orchestral music
40. Prado site
42. Sing the praises of
43. Wool cap
44. Jolie's youngest daughter
45. Go AWOL
48. Painter of *Odalisque with Magnolias*
50. Seam reinforcements
51. Legalese adverb
52. A Great Lake
53. Fabric protectors
57. Caustic substance
58. Touched down
59. Sabbatical, e.g.
60. Suggestive look
61. Eleanor's successor
62. Man of memorable marbles

DOWN

1. Sarnoff's corp.
2. What Ann Sheridan had
3. Remolded Clay?
4. "Me too"
5. Great divides
6. Spaces in the forest
7. In the future
8. Completed
9. Word in a Tolstoy title
10. *The Bank Dick* bartender
11. Singer Perry and kin
12. Eastern princes
13. Control device
18. Between, in Brussels
21. Out of trim
22. Horse pill
23. Eared seal

Solution is on page 230

24. Freq. retirement destination
25. Princess' irritant
27. Destined beginning?
29. Thomas Paine, notably
30. Famous trio
31. Hounds' quarry
32. Pointed arch
34. Give succor
36. Actress Rehan
38. Bireme power
39. Praline ingredient
40. Dura or alma follower
41. Easy to like
43. Fortuneteller's cards
45. Reside
46. Fueling fear
47. *Ghostbusters* ooze
48. Ancient Egypt's capital
49. Madame de —
51. Denver's skipper
53. Hack
54. Fall behind
55. Pompey's 56
56. Hatch or Hutchison: abbr.

by Cathy Millhauser

ACROSS

1. *The Lion King* hero
6. Playwright Connelly
10. Bard's jet?
14. Song syllables
15. Switch back?
16. Wally and Beaver's mom
17. Dough for shaving supplies?
19. Latin "Behold!"
20. Roscoe of *Gone With the Wind*
21. Cost of a tube of ChapStick?
23. Cat breed
25. People-food morsels
26. Marked down
29. Chinese canines, for sort
32. Pizzeria wafts
35. Coll. in Ypsilanti
37. Baker or Battle, e.g.
38. Bled or fled
39. Egotistic
42. Classic counter-moving game
43. Article
45. Clique
46. Pain in the neck
48. Apollo's birthplace
50. Nod of approval
52. Old Age
54. Grown sans chemicals
58. Billfold arrangement?
62. Marvin Gaye's singing daughter
63. Inventor's germ
64. Beach admission charge?
66. Ambivalent
67. Fatigue
68. Was atilt
69. Actress Martinelli
70. Hoosegow
71. Units of force

DOWN

1. Sam Browne belt part
2. Incensed
3. Large goblet
4. Flourish
5. Bern's river
6. *Never on Sunday* star Mercouri
7. Doesn't give — (ceases to care)
8. Esmeralda's tribe
9. Women's mag
10. Expelled
11. Cheap jazz drum set?
12. Formerly
13. Eterne's opposite
18. They have their orders
22. Sculptor Hans
24. Balin and Claire
27. Sinister turns

Solution is on page 230

28. Br. record label
30. The Shadow knows it
31. *Idem*
32. Thirst-provoking
33. Deserve
34. This puzzle's theme entries?
36. Escorted down the aisle
40. Grazing place
41. Nail head?
44. *Orlando Furioso* sorceress
47. Tool brand
49. Helios' Roman counterpart
51. Metal shop material
53. Cozy retreats
55. First name in no-hitters
56. Vacuous
57. Outdoor market sights
58. Locus
59. Tiki, e.g.
60. Dijon deed
61. Cross inscription
65. Declining

by Bob Sefick

ACROSS

1. Good belt
5. Stipends
9. Sing the blues
13. Sweet-sounding Horne
14. Fa-—
15. Porridge in the nursery?
16. Long-eared mammals
18. Maternal kin
19. Irish goddess of the arts
20. Office chatter
22. Corrodes
24. Poison gases
25. '50s dropouts
29. Impasse
30. TV maker
31. Party poopers
33. Scorer's info
36. Svgs. setups
38. Pass in the legislature
40. Literally, "gathering place"
41. Three-dimensional, in a way
43. Milkmaid's perch
45. Stimpy's sidekick
46. Med. school course
48. Achilles heel
50. *Los — Unidos*
53. Mild
54. Covered, at sea
56. This evening, in ads
60. Blatant
61. Tall-stemmed plant
63. Charles and Ephron
64. Row
65. "…I could — horse!"
66. Nation's allies
67. Greek peak
68. Judge

DOWN

1. Generous portion
2. Model, perhaps
3. Golgotha inscription
4. Grown-up's toy
5. Driver's annoyance
6. It has a hammer and an anvil
7. Some fraternity members
8. The bird in *Peter and the Wolf*
9. Entered
10. Consumer-friendly orgs.
11. Basket fiber
12. St. David's Day symbols
15. Nehi alternatives
17. Gastronomical delight
21. Royal symbol
23. Trapper's supply
25. —-a-brac

Solution is on page 230

26. Neutral shade

27. Pocket radio power

28. Cold-shoulder causes

32. Move it

34. Lt. Kojak

35. They are, to Theodosius

37. "Somethin' Stupid" pair

39. Two-thirds of a WWII film

42. Student body at the Citadel

44. Detroit dud

47. Miner's measure

49. Caught on

50. Federal issue for savers

51. Relish

52. "From — shining…"

55. Location for a luminary

57. *Dies* —

58. Shopper's bag

59. Waxed treat

62. Matter, to the judge

by Janet Bender

ACROSS

1. Level
5. Satisfy, and then some
9. Flash
14. Turgenev's birthplace
15. Kudos from Shalit
16. Temporary hair coloring
17. My denial about going to a Bronx ballpark
20. Tore
21. Scottish explorer John
22. Phil Rizzuto nickname
26. Tangle in a net
30. Originates
31. Sponsor of the Missouri Compromise
32. Lobster coral
33. *The Duino Elegies* poet
34. It precedes *tav*
35. Put away
36. Floridians' advice to catcher McCarver
39. *Iolanthe* chorus member
40. Iditarod terminus
41. Little Miss Dinsmore
43. Western Hemisphere gp.
44. Pack it in
45. Gets on one's nerves
46. Performed plainsong
48. Offerings from Greg Maddux
49. In defense of
50. Actor Hersholt
51. Pleased reaction to a Celtics win
59. Disturbed
60. — *plaisir* (gladly)
61. Wrap for Holyfield
62. Very, very small
63. Simple
64. Way out

DOWN

1. McCarthy aide Cohn
2. First name in coaching
3. Koan poser
4. Wapiti
5. Brunch choice
6. Holography device
7. Roman elegist
8. "Owner of a Lonely Heart" group
9. Like pomade
10. Compare
11. Alpine river
12. Super-secret spy org.
13. Novelist Josephine
18. High regard
19. Early Verdi opera
22. Patriotic org.
23. From southern Ukraine
24. Most Heeplike
25. *Ship of Fools'* Werner

Solution is on page 230

26. *Crème de la crème*
27. Skilled sculptor
28. More commodious
29. Soldier/novelist Wallace
31. Munch with gusto
34. Prepared to sing the national anthem
35. Bar offering
37. Summer employee
38. Wool variety
39. Then, in Turin
42. Dangerous curve
44. Like a social climber
45. Furtive look
47. Time and again
48. Where Exodus is read
50. All that jazz
51. "Life is — a dream…"
52. Unclose, poetically
53. Chicago-Atlanta dir.
54. Hoover, for one
55. It's past *due*
56. Red or White follower
57. Sapporo sash
58. Lay odds

by Matt Gaffney

ACROSS

1. Maryland college athlete
5. *Bugsy* setting
10. Pt. of DC
14. Alimony recipients
15. Kate Nelligan role
16. Pitcher
17. Western Samoa's capital
18. Marching style
20. Roy Orbison song
22. Treat wrongly
23. Adviser Carnegie
24. Monopoly purchase
27. Tyke
28. Novelist Rand
29. Account book
34. It washes down eels
38. It's not gross
39. Brian Benben series
41. Buck Rogers portrayer Gerard
42. Sea bordering Crimea
44. Odor
45. Union leaver
46. Crunch target
48. Exotic fruit
50. Competent
52. Shammy cloths
56. Tontine recipients
60. Silver load
61. Edible pocket
63. Role for Harrison
64. Like neon
65. Czech/German river
66. Eleanor's successor
67. Area for a joust
68. Tom, Dick or Harry

DOWN

1. Leaves for breakfast
2. Big show
3. Bit part
4. Job follower
5. Three-piece suit parts
6. Nobelist Root
7. Characteristic carriers
8. Ulterior motive
9. Iowa landscape feature
10. "Dewey — Truman" (notable blooper)
11. *White Album* song
12. Stress researcher Hans
13. *Uno + due*
19. Skeleton starter
21. Triangular traffic sign
24. Tennis player Mandlikova
25. Courtroom cry
26. Golden rule word
27. Cheat sheet
30. Picks a dud
31. Wallace of *E.T.*

Solution is on page 231

32. Ubiquitous mall store
33. Ostrich's cousin
35. Indian tourist mecca
36. St. Vladimir's dukedom
37. Portoferraio's island
40. Beersheba's locale
43. Peak counterparts
47. Boilermaker half
49. Grand Slam part
50. In unison
51. They're traded and analyzed
52. Most Egyptian Muslims
53. Yens
54. Three-time Wimbledon winner
55. Greenery purchases
57. Embark
58. Baltic Sea gulf
59. Skiing turn
60. Bodleian, for one: abbr.
62. Is following you?

by Martin Ashwood-Smith

ACROSS

1. Take to the cleaners
6. Toil away
10. Gumbo
14. — Haute
15. Hawaiian for "new moon"
16. Dill, in the Bible
17. Matriculate
18. — the finish
19. Run-of-the-mill
20. Start of a quotation
23. Wise guys
24. Galileo and his compatriots
26. Genes designer?
27. Early synthesizer
29. Comment from Cratchit's boss
30. Stare in astonishment
33. Middle of the quotation
35. "With the jawbone of —…"
37. One of Magda's sisters
38. Knack
39. Author of the quotation
41. Salt Lake City team
42. Form ending
43. Minimum wage, e.g.
44. Exists, to Einstein
46. Rake
48. Natural land bridge
52. End of the quotation
55. Papal name
56. Kind of frost
57. *Ars —, vita brevis*
58. Ladies' man
59. Pound of poetry
60. Krupp's city
61. Barker in the movies
62. Come-hither
63. Unembellished

DOWN

1. Goethe's love
2. Consequently
3. Tapestry town
4. Concierge's station
5. Inform against
6. Deadly blades
7. Palmist's concern
8. e.e. cummings' "i sing of — glad and big"
9. Deteriorate
10. Hops-drying houses
11. Be aware of
12. An echo chamber increases it
13. From — Z
21. Nest-egg acct.

Solution is on page 231

22. Fitting
25. Peacock Throne occupants
27. It's in the can in Cannes
28. — impulse
30. Range
31. Symbolist's stock in trade
32. Universal rival
33. Heart of the matter
34. Antarctica, directionwise
36. Fancy fiddle
40. Vigils
44. Pt. of RI
45. Steps across hedgerows
47. Leaf vein
48. "— for no man but myself" (*Timon of Athens*)
49. Bright bunch
50. Madison's roommate
51. Smelt fishy?
53. Percolate
54. "You Bet Your Life" host
55. Drivers' org.?

71 HEAD FOR THE HILLS!

by Richard Thomas

ACROSS

1. Mr. Ed's foot
5. Final Four round
10. Sharp sound
14. Whet spot
15. Pamphlet
16. He wears a white hat
17. Hills
20. Fakery
21. Nail polish color
22. Ten C-notes
23. Regal rod
24. Stanislavsky's system
28. Bucko
29. Bathymetry milieu
30. Mini Indy car
31. Fin. plans
35. Hills
38. Overfill
39. Toward the sunrise
40. Vital vessel
41. Wicked glower
42. Malice
43. Totem makers
47. Caesar of note
48. Mrs. Robinson's daughter
49. Vision aids
54. Hills
56. Dextrous beginning
57. Investigate
58. *Come Back, Little Sheba* playwright
59. Origin
60. Take the helm
61. Mound of earth

DOWN

1. Fiber plant
2. Whiff
3. *Oeillade*
4. Yard parts
5. Blotto
6. Notched
7. Queen takes king, perhaps
8. R.R. regulator
9. Violin part marking
10. Parakeet's tweet
11. "— Be"
12. Sprung up
13. Gondolier
18. "Shoo!"
19. Door hole
23. Deficient
24. Swarms
25. Guayaquil's country: abbr.
26. Camp sight
27. Food fish
28. Buckle

Solution is on page 231

30. Hoaxes

31. "White Wedding" rocker

32. Philatelically valuable

33. Kitty starter

34. Jazzman Getz

36. Hits the car ahead

37. Chihuahua, e.g.

41. Siberian stream

42. Confession participant

43. French equivalent of the Oscar

44. Bowie's battle

45. Hercules for our time?

46. Drop in on

47. Italian wine

49. "Swinging on a Star" beast

50. Plagiarism

51. Bowler's alley

52. MIT grad, perhaps

53. Part of a pocket watch

55. Form of coal

by Peter Snow

ACROSS

1. Last of a series
6. Chip's partner
10. Settles on (with "for")
14. Surviving specimen
15. Dutch treat
16. Knowledge
17. Vigilant
18. Goldbrick
19. Earl of Avon
20. Exhausting
22. Crisp cottons
24. Oasts
26. Travolta movie
27. Wraps
30. Give a lift to
32. Box at the opera
33. Tropical tuber
35. Plus
39. Bobble a ball
40. Battery companion
42. M. Malraux
43. Musicologist Taylor
45. Agile
46. Greek cheese
47. In unison
49. Gapes
51. Vector's opposite
54. Diaphanous
56. Purplish-red garnet
58. New York skaters
62. Taunt
63. Enthusiastic
65. Accounting reference
66. Muslim commander
67. Mah-jongg piece
68. Part of T.S.E.
69. Clears
70. Part of BPOE
71. Musical signs

DOWN

1. Toward the mouth
2. Hawaiian chant
3. Au, e.g.: abbr.
4. Ornamental candleholder
5. On a roll
6. Vouchsafe
7. Total
8. *Symphonie Espagnole* composer
9. Come into view
10. Evergreen shrubs
11. Daises
12. Timber
13. Have a hunch
21. Lays an egg?
23. Eminent
25. Abrades
27. Iditarod vehicle
28. Ripped

Solution is on page 231

29. Grimm monster

31. "…frets his —
upon the stage"
(*Macbeth*)

34. League: abbr.

36. Workshop item

37. Art deco great

38. Oriental shrubs

40. Musical direction

41. Gets better,
medically
speaking

44. Equine ailment

46. Lively French
dance

48. Like Versailles

50. Cable car

51. *Bonjour Tristesse*
author

52. "Love…no season
knows, nor —"
(Donne)

53. Scope

55. Pelts

57. Maleficent

59. Yale men

60. Insurrection

61. Tipplers

64. Class

73 ANXIETY ATTACK

by Matt Gaffney

ACROSS

1. "Blondie" creator Young
5. Radio's countdown man
10. Slick
13. Mercury or Saturn, e.g.
14. Ancient Roman port
15. European silk center
17. Big Apple expression of gratitude
19. *The Samurai* author
20. — Tots
21. Himalayan sights
23. They keep on running
26. Beatles' record company
27. It's furthest from the point
28. Congregation
31. Knickerbockers, e.g.
32. Wall flowers, sometimes?
33. Pose
36. "Need You Tonight" group
37. Devoured
38. It can get pretty sticky
39. Dow drop
40. Lucknow's land
41. Track runner
42. Easy to miss
44. Visited
45. Ludicrous
47. Chills
48. Most trifling
50. Latin for "there is lacking"
51. Lowell and Grant
52. Egyptian curse
57. Type of furnishings
58. Garlic-flavored mayonnaise
59. Give the go-ahead
60. Take back the go-ahead
61. Capitalize on again
62. Mercedes-—

DOWN

1. Fleet member
2. "And — begat Uri, and Uri begat…" (1 Chronicles)
3. Onetime Klugman costar
4. Promos, often
5. Sweathogs' teacher
6. *Angela's* —
7. Night light
8. Augsburg article
9. Ankle-length
10. Is dormant
11. Row of wildcats
12. Sing in Appenzell
16. Breathtaking object?
18. Lines to measure abscissas
22. Fee to go free

146

Solution is on page 232

23. Lacking enthusiasm
24. From Shiraz
25. Feline esophageal connection
28. Work, as hours
29. Specialty
30. Controlled
32. Showed up at
34. Retinue

35. Bingolike games
37. BASIC command
38. "Congrats!"
40. April 13, e.g.
41. Modem kin
43. Basically, to Brutus
44. Quarterback Kosar
45. The man in the Iran mosque

46. Certain lion's home
47. Banisters
49. Peter or Paul
50. Third dynasty of China
53. Total wealth, figuratively
54. Alibi of baseball
55. A Bobbsey
56. Affair of 1797

147

74 CUE ME IN

by Rich Norris

ACROSS

1. Holds for hoods
6. Oversimplified ideas
9. Water carrier
13. Forearm bones
14. "If — a Hammer"
16. Mars' dark part
17. Some Oscar winners
20. Driver's license abbr.
21. Productive
22. Show contempt for
23. Tenor
25. Rathskeller request
26. In any way
28. Political ploys
33. To — (everyone)
36. Don Knotts negative
38. Jane Curtin role

39. Timesaving tab splitter
42. Strut with vanity
43. Old Roman route
44. Gyro bread
45. Highly passionate
47. Corp. honchos
49. Rabble-rouse
51. Small space between leaf veins
55. Takes for granted
59. Winter woe
60. USSR successor
61. Chef's creations
64. First name in fashion
65. On the horizon
66. Draped garment
67. Visa alternative, for short
68. German connector
69. Discharge

DOWN

1. Wynonna and Naomi
2. Thrown for —
3. Nightmares
4. Bolt from the blues?
5. Deem appropriate
6. Aniston's old flame
7. "So!"
8. Separate a sentence
9. Lead Qatarist?
10. Hoopster Frazier
11. Writer Bombeck
12. Others
15. Force units
18. Afloat
19. Ceremonious
24. More offensive
25. Puffed up
27. Places
29. Go by

Solution is on page 232

30. High: prefix

31. Kind of act

32. Wheys

33. Scheduled mtg.

34. Italian politico Aldo

35. Maple genus

37. Multitheater conclusion?

40. Tough nut to crack

41. Panacea

46. Movers and shakers

48. Wander about

50. Shakespearean start

52. September shade

53. Some bar brews

54. Positive influence

55. Legend maker

56. Urban eyesore

57. Support (with "with")

58. DOS alternative

59. Manage

62. Benny's Wilson

63. Kind of law or order

by Francis Heaney

ACROSS

1. BMI counterpart
6. H.H. Munro
10. Tanka or rondel
14. Stone monument
15. Rara follower
16. — *jure*
17. Trig ratio
18. Solidarity's Walesa
19. Deed
20. Latrop?
22. Shake hands on it
23. Leonowens' adoptive land
24. Temporarily inactive
26. First cardinal?
29. Geol. or biol.
30. "No —!" ("Sure!")
31. Medieval
33. Neologisms
37. Where the pois are
38. Chihuahua *ciao*
40. The Censor
41. Trapped
43. Marshall Islands test site
45. Prefix on an Ocean Spray label
46. Patriotic org.
47. Popeye, e.g.
48. One sensitive to the arts
51. Square, for one
53. Unkempt ones
54. Emil?
59. Mitchell mansion
60. Fall flat
61. Black nightshade
62. Ear-related
63. Type type: abbr.
64. Old-womanly
65. Eat like a bird?
66. Depend
67. Folklorist Zora — Hurston

DOWN

1. *The Nazarene* author
2. Where Menander meandered
3. It's in France
4. Baldwin and Guinness
5. Board game from India
6. Deli choice
7. "— *plaisir!*"
8. Oklahoma tribe
9. Somewhat: suffix
10. Eot?
11. Battle field?
12. German ironworks center
13. Polyphonic vocal composition
21. Vegas game
22. Age
25. Queensland capital
26. Eye

Solution is on page 232

27. Subject or object, usually

28. Greek letters

32. Aedi?

33. Spanish hero (with "the")

34. Carriage

35. Sicilian prone to outbursts?

36. Saint-Étienne evening

39. Contradict

42. Aphrodite's consort

44. Tony Stark's alter ego

46. Squint

48. Bar at the bar

49. Blue hue

50. Doughnut-shaped

52. Steakhouse selection

55. Coin of Kashan

56. Highlight of 11-Down

57. Hermit's hut

58. *Death and Fire* painter

60. Tree of the genus *Abies*

by Matt Gaffney

ACROSS

1. From Apia
7. Dartmoor structure
11. Vaughn and Udall
14. Slip by
15. Mathematical correspondence
16. Bright
17. Fosse biopic
19. Swell spot?
20. Guitarist Lofgren
21. Tops
22. Nonflowering embryophyte
23. Get
24. President Karimov's constituents
26. Bummer
27. Best Director of '86 and '89
29. Kepler contemporary
30. Multiflavored seasoning

35. Use a shuttle
36. Nighttime photography pioneer
40. Flivver
41. Site of Burgoyne's surrender
42. Gilded images
44. Goneril's victim
47. Say nay to
48. Incalculable
52. Hunk's asset
54. Where *les cheveux* grow
55. Trim
56. Regarding
57. Palindromic preposition
58. Minor college exam
61. Moral misdeed
62. Bumpers of the Senate
63. Journalist's in
64. Baseball's Kluszewski

65. Harts
66. Duke of Cooperstown

DOWN

1. O'Casey and O'Kelly
2. Supporters
3. Chisel driver
4. Decides
5. Butt bit
6. Teachers' org.
7. Paragon of toy soldiers
8. Built like —
9. Flows gently
10. Oft-wed celeb
11. Mistral Spider maker
12. Stovepipe
13. *"Desafinado"* Grammy winner
18. It's picked up in bars
22. SSS initiator

Solution is on page 232

24. Save

25. Dobie's pursuer

28. Bireme equipment

29. Cadged

31. Lith., once

32. Bake sale gp.

33. Chicago sch.

34. Rank below thane

36. Proof of value

37. Banks of Buffalo

38. Type of alignment

39. Straggle

43. Humorist Edgar Wilson

45. Crazy

46. Announcement

48. Radii neighbors

49. '60 Wimbledon champ Fraser

50. Spud

51. One of *Two Virgins*

53. One who nods off

56. Here, in Hidalgo

58. Come to a conclusion

59. Eds. work with them

60. Over there

by Randall Hartman

ACROSS

1. Muslim pilgrimage
5. Irons' voice in *The Lion King*
9. Mothers of Invention leader
14. Lamb's other name
15. Plank from the *Mayflower*
16. Olivia's *Captain Blood* costar
17. Evelyn Waugh's brother
18. Unkn.
19. Ancient Attic assembly
20. Balky Cervantes character?
22. Drop
23. Hoskins, in *Hook*
24. Voyage starter
25. Knocked one's block off
28. Rooms for pounds
30. Average
33. Take effect
34. Hideout
35. Canon's Yeoman's offering
36. Headstrong Tarzan creator?
39. Sticky place?
40. Shout to Gantry
41. Bar patron's order
42. Alway
43. Laugh a minute
44. Put down
45. Meditative philosophy
46. Obsess over (with "on")
47. Scatter's accompaniment
50. Burdened painter of *Reptiles*?
55. Treasure
56. Ill-considered
57. Appearance
58. "It ain't over till it's over" utterer
59. *Salida del sol* direction
60. Trigger's check
61. Rye fungus
62. A couple of bucks?
63. Put on the Rit

DOWN

1. Costumer Edith
2. French phone greeting
3. — Bien Phu
4. Spillikin
5. Convinced
6. Sacajawea's craft, maybe
7. "There's — to be said for…"
8. Filmmaker Clair
9. Extremist
10. Incandescent bulb element
11. Ski tip
12. Epidermal opening
13. Like Pegasus
21. Fatima descendant
24. Snippy remark
25. *Résistance* unit?

Solution is on page 233

26. Brooke's ex
27. Marilyn's *Some Like It Hot* role
28. Aspect
29. Collateral of a sort
30. Diagram grammatically
31. Kauai "hi"
32. Bow application
34. Wheels of fortune?

35. It can take a trick
37. Precipitate
38. PC mavens
43. Say again
44. Dancer's partner
45. He left his mark on things
46. Rush
47. Zaharias of the links

48. Hessian river
49. Connors' '76 U.S. Open opponent
50. Ozzie and Harriet's '60s sitcom competitor
51. Example
52. — Lewis and the News
53. Presque Isle's lake
54. Transvaal coin

by Frances Burton

ACROSS

1. Go to great pains?
5. Martial artist Jackie
9. Qualified
13. Water fall
14. Menelaus' mate
16. Aura
17. Archer of films
18. One of Liz's exes
19. Slowly move
20. Lettuce mound
21. neerg?
23. Jack up
25. Waterproof boots
26. Huge, in Huelva
28. Mountain greenery
30. Charters
31. Janis Joplin sobriquet
32. Dynasty that introduced Buddhism in China
35. Thrice less twice
36. Footprint
37. Drawing card
38. Distress
39. Everyday language
40. Rashness
41. Palm off (with "on")
42. Leash
43. Violoncello master
46. Fur seal's mates
47. dnomaid?
50. Mined-over matter
53. Norman conquest?
54. Pungent spice
55. Fresh
56. Number lost
57. Waxed wick
58. It's passed from generation to generation
59. Grafted, in heraldry
60. Puts down on paper
61. Places for pupils

DOWN

1. Child of the streets
2. Vaudeville prop
3. ward?
4. Vane dir.
5. Curds sans whey
6. Skirt the issue
7. Gershwin portrayer in *Rhapsody in Blue*
8. The Kerbys' Saint Bernard
9. Docket
10. Man about town
11. Also-ran
12. Spouted vessels
15. Faye Dunaway film
21. Tops
22. Countess' husband
24. Pay to play
26. Fill out

Solution is on page 233

27. Separation location

28. Spread

29. Add a dash of mash

31. Good points

32. kcik?

33. Talent, in Taranto

34. At no time, in rhyme

36. Cut into certain bears' shares

37. Past due

39. Head count

40. "Take it!"

41. *Femme* follower

42. Those agreeable

43. Lader's load

44. Home run king

45. Shorebird

46. Port in a storm

48. Stick or dash starter

49. "No way!"

51. Russo of Hollywood

52. Meadow mamas

55. Deteriorate, in a way

by Robert Wolfe

ACROSS

1. Cut out
5. Mimics Mel
10. Appeared
14. Droop
15. Kind of code
16. Steel component
17. Sal's canal
18. Amongst, in Avignon
19. It's inherited
20. United States
23. Sea patterns
24. Alum
25. Whup
28. Stripling
29. Sidekick
31. Greek civic goddess
33. Meted out
38. United States
42. Political doer
43. Service word
44. Majoli of tennis
45. Sch. organization
48. Where Hope was born: abbr.
49. Rope fiber
52. True up
54. United States
60. Inflamed
61. Actress Massey
62. On the safe side
63. Tilted
64. Made fast
65. Catch in the act
66. Word on the street?
67. Thomas Luck's creator
68. Parsley kin

DOWN

1. Aviated
2. Singer of *Footloose*
3. Bulldog fans
4. Choose
5. — Buck (Derby winner)
6. Perfumed
7. Those against
8. Mountain lake
9. Use a pung
10. Castro's Cohiba, e.g.
11. Amphitheater's center
12. One-celled organism
13. Ethyl ending
21. Tintoretto's tint
22. Northern hemisphere?
25. Kenyan river
26. Kim's ex
27. Small amphibian
29. Arafat's org.
30. Aggregate
32. 29-Across, in Tours

Solution is on page 233

33. Seem
34. Refrain syllable
35. Uninspiring
36. Earl of Avon
37. Viet dollar
39. Madonna role
40. LXX ÷ V
41. "There — tavern…"
45. Orrery component
46. Harangue
47. Even one
49. Half a college cheer
50. Ohio city
51. Sawed wood
52. Love affair
53. Antelope of Ethiopia
55. Lofty
56. Spicy stew
57. Kyrgyzstani range
58. Diamond or Simon
59. Bowery Boy Gabriel
60. Arm of the mil.

159

by Alex Vaughn

ACROSS

1. Eight bits
5. Early TV jungle man
10. — ben Adhem
14. Sounds of amazement
15. Waitress at Mel's
16. Fingerprints, Brit-style
17. Ukulele and Alibi
18. Current events?
19. Galbraith's subj.
20. Wallace or Wasserman
21. Even
22. "Mind if — suggestion?"
24. Prefix with bond or dollar
26. Lapis follower
28. They sing the bum-bums
30. Emulate Tina Brown
31. Chill

34. Nervous
35. Aim a finger
36. Prufrock creator's monogram
37. Stratum
38. Unclarify?
39. Mr. Bill's wail
40. Neighbor of Jor.
41. Tailor's tucks
42. Antigone's uncle
43. Ex-NHLer Dryden
44. Coy
45. Searches
46. "Let the punishment — crime"
48. Bear in the air
49. Actress Matlin
51. Laugh a minute
53. Corporate alias abbr.
56. Reserve
57. Fowl place
59. Yemeni capital
60. — *Lucasta*

61. Rub out
62. Spread like butter?
63. Adjusts
64. Yo-yos
65. "Smoke Gets in Your Eyes" composer

DOWN

1. See red
2. Ox-cessory?
3. Remarque location
4. Serpentine letter
5. Proportions
6. "It's a Sin to Tell —"
7. Moderate
8. Expert
9. Fitting anew
10. "Let's Make —"
11. Autry location
12. Double-reed
13. Annapolis initials

Solution is on page 233

21. Deuce beater
23. Jeff's pal
25. CIS predecessor
27. *Ciao*, in Chiapas
28. It's to dye for
29. Fennel kin
32. Response to 52-Down
33. Punjabi police

35. See 57-Across
38. Like Smetana's bride
39. Mined-over matter
41. Go with
42. Brusque
45. Repeats a passage
47. Actress Chase's namesakes

49. Wharton grads, e.g.
50. Tops
52. Response to 32-Down
54. It has a head and hops
55. Unkn.
58. Gold, to García
59. Status report from *Atlantis*

by Richard Silvestri

ACROSS

1. Some *Mariners'* destination
5. Everly Brothers song
10. Big deal at the Taj Mahal?
14. City on the Oka
15. Animated
16. Crazed
17. First name in mysteries
18. Early physician
19. Part of a chorus line?
20. Spot cummings at last
23. Kyoto quaff
24. Winter feeder fare
25. Charge
26. Part of TGIF
27. Couric of TV news
30. Show place?
32. Collier's lode
34. — mater (brain membrane)
35. Pod pellet

36. Mr. or Mrs., e.g.
38. Zorro's black stallion
42. Summertime slaker
43. Where east met west, in the sky
44. Had no doubt
45. Cast's supporter, at times
48. Arrogant
50. Enzyme suffix
51. Descartes' conclusion
52. School near Windsor Castle
54. Opal ending
56. Censor AARP bulletin
61. On the up and up
62. Ness adversary
63. Opposite of exo-
64. Cork location
65. NBA '93 Rookie of the Year
66. 1963 Pulitzer-winning biographer

67. Smell a lot
68. Magnetic beginning
69. Good, clean fun

DOWN

1. Homer Simpson's hangout
2. Took in
3. Let out
4. Elegant
5. Stuffing spice
6. Norway's July 29 honoree
7. Region in southern Poland
8. Baltic, on the board
9. Tooth, in Tuscany
10. White House Scottie
11. Gulf of Salerno port
12. Painter's brush, of sorts
13. Signed off on
21. Cry in the comics

Solution is on page 234

22. Out-and-out
26. Keogh kin
28. Area behind the altar
29. Sit backwards
31. Actor Azaria
33. Funny Lebowitz
35. Political patronage
37. Landscaper's tool
38. Sign of stress
39. Boa
40. Apostate
41. Use plastic
43. Hydra, for one
45. Jeanne, to James Cagney
46. Performance artist Anderson
47. Tainted
48. Right-triangle ratio
49. "Owner of a Lonely Heart" group
53. Approaching the hour
55. Sheffield shipment
57. Glimpse
58. Castor or Pollux
59. Forage storage
60. Meringue maker's leftover

by Thomas Schier

ACROSS

1. Actress Hagen
4. New York City
10. Tricked
13. Swig
15. '60s adaptation of *The Four Poster*
16. Cooler cooler
17. Wave-tracking record
19. Haggard heroine
20. South American plain
21. *Father of the Bride* author
23. Chinese puzzle
26. Inner: prefix
27. "Raven" beauty
30. *I, Claudius* attire
33. Angry reaction
36. — about
37. Tear open
38. "Do Ya" rockers
39. Word puzzle
41. Recollection collection
42. Cravat kin
44. Two-sided
45. Some CPR givers
46. Cosmetics
47. Mail, as an entry
49. Commemorative poems
51. Knotted up
55. Purplish-red colors
59. Rhône tributary
60. My and thy
61. Fingerprint
64. Grille cover
65. Philippic
66. Opposite of 26-Across
67. Sweet spud
68. Province NW of Madrid
69. DDE opponent

DOWN

1. Carpenter's double-nutter
2. Magnetic induction unit
3. Highway to the North
4. Evans of jazz
5. "Deep Space Nine" changeling
6. Jerkin and jumpsuit, e.g.
7. "Java" man
8. On — (as a challenge)
9. Impetus
10. Frequency distribution chart
11. Take great pains?
12. Salt lick licker
14. Prickly sensation
18. Erudition
22. Orwell's alma mater
24. By and by
25. Indivisible units
28. Vagabond
29. Describing 28-Down
31. "Is too!" rebuttal

Solution is on page 234

32. Resorts to exercise?
33. Lop the crop
34. Rick's love
35. Group interaction chart
39. Take care of
40. Chessman portrayer
43. Billow, in Blois

45. Tie up
48. Not — many words
50. Flight necessity
52. Author Federico García
53. Maternally related
54. Musicians' samples

55. Dick of whaling fiction
56. Psychic sighting
57. It's a lot for your money
58. With 63-Down, Spider-Man creator
62. FB's gains
63. See 58-Down

83 EGO TRIP

by D.J. DeChristopher

ACROSS

1. Pedantic ones
6. Pistons great Thomas
11. Knighthood's rules
14. Recite
15. Kurt Waldheim, for one
16. Blue — (*Yellow Submarine* baddie)
17. Verbal communication gp.
18. Cairo natives: abbr.
19. Torn of "The Larry Sanders Show"
20. Atty.'s degree
21. Actor Wood and namesakes
23. Diary passage
25. Besprinkle
26. Agt.'s cut
27. "— Three Lives"
30. Run-in
32. Bathsheba's spouse
34. Norman, for one
35. He cat
36. Cell unit
37. Fran Fine's best friend
38. Down under, at sea
40. Tampico total
41. Biblical wall word
42. Rake
43. QB gains
44. Litter's littlest
46. Inventor Nikola
48. Invest with authority
51. N.T. book
53. Towel inscription
54. Caustic cleaner
55. Cadmus' daughter
56. *Monty Python's — Brian*
58. Unites
60. Pointed
61. "She moves —, and she looks a queen" (*Iliad* translation)
62. Seasons
63. Filled with the latest info

DOWN

1. Pers.
2. "And what is so — a day …"
3. Inspirational ego trip of song and cinema
4. It ain't hay
5. Near-def.
6. All thumbs
7. Paddington or Penn
8. 007's ego trip
9. Indigo shrub
10. Live by
11. Appeared

Solution is on page 234

12. Pea pod
13. Orator's ego trip
14. Enlistee's ego trip
19. Change one's tune
22. Project
24. Relieve
26. Atom's binding forces
28. Author Hunter
29. Chip's crony
30. Night light
31. Charles' sport
33. Morgenstern and Penmark
39. Minuscule
41. L–P link
45. Topples
47. Chances
48. Panegyric
49. Tolkien creatures
50. Supremes being?
51. Music theorist's notes
52. Craving to eat odd substances
57. Consume
58. Is competent
59. Ice-cream maker

by Randall Hartman

ACROSS

1. Motion preceder
5. *The Mill on the —*
10. Cager O'Neal, informally
14. Part of
15. Play devil's advocate, perhaps
16. "To Sir With Love" singer
17. Jupiter's counterpart
18. Fragrant seed
19. Narwhal
20. 1965 Sinatra war drama?
23. Medium for Matisse
25. Peaked
26. Up for discussion: abbr.
27. "— to the West Wind"
28. Like a straight shot
31. Hound sound
33. Gwen on Broadway, in the '50s
35. Nastase of tennis
37. Calcutta currency
41. Enigma to Godwin Austen?
44. Played over
45. Alpine goat
46. Emulated Rumpelstiltskin
47. Sgt. or cpl.
49. Dried out in Durango
51. Short byway?
52. Indy's quest
55. "Gotcha!"
57. Comes after
59. Observation from John Donne?
63. Sleeve cards
64. Kidneylike
65. Space start
68. Spirit
69. Scheme
70. Feel in one's bones
71. *Siegfried* role
72. Pegasus, for one
73. Windsor Castle neighbor

DOWN

1. She played Cleo
2. 1969 Three Dog Night smash
3. High school help
4. Assault
5. Munich miss
6. Shrovetide follower
7. Last writes
8. Bar order
9. Stern
10. Asperse
11. Chinese province
12. "Stayin' —"
13. Bogart in *The Caine Mutiny*
21. *Good Will Hunting*'s Affleck
22. Brief gaps
23. Opposite

Solution is on page 234

24. Hopi dwelling
29. Kyrgyzstan range
30. Poitier's *In the Heat of the Night* role
32. Dogpatch dads
34. *— Called Horse*
36. "Waiting for the Robert —"
38. Rash
39. Quick-fry
40. Jackson and Jeffreys
42. Machu Picchu residents
43. Stood out
48. John and Maureen
50. *Boy — Dolphin*
52. Knock the socks off of
53. Formula 1 car
54. Massage
56. As regards
58. Bushmaster, e.g.
60. *— de Pascua*
61. 1953 Pulitzer Prize winner
62. Sotheby's action
66. Baby bounder
67. "On My —" (LaBelle/McDonald hit)

by Mel Rosen

ACROSS

1. Except
5. Gives as surety
10. Hummus holder
14. Marlene's *Blue Angel* costar
15. Confederate foe
16. Genetic carriers
17. Short orchestral work
19. Box for baubles
20. Molasses
21. Seam inserts
23. Beatitude
24. More appropriate
25. British school
27. Galleon feature
28. Gluck and namesakes
31. FBI agent
32. Indiana's pursuit
33. Purport
34. Height: prefix
35. Fugue introduction
37. Zuider or Tappan
38. Grounds
40. Nincompoop
41. Poet Pound
42. Tooth: prefix
43. "Yo!" in old Rome
44. Seth's son
45. Musical Brewer
47. Hirsute prefix
48. "Western" dishes
50. Pop music's 10,000 —
54. Filibuster target
55. Fanciful composition
57. Actress Raines
58. Wroth
59. One-third of a Byrds hit
60. 88 Earth days, on Mercury
61. Perfume
62. Borax, for one

DOWN

1. Zen is one
2. Cupid
3. Hollywood crosser
4. San Diego's neighbor
5. Hurly-—
6. Pay up
7. Sundial time
8. Greater in duration
9. Shakespearean tinker
10. Create demand
11. Light entr'acte
12. Stretched
13. Bargain's tag words
18. M. Friedman's forte: abbr.
22. Like a tough cookie?
24. Near Eastern sweet
25. Toastmaster

Solution is on page 235

26. Italian folk dance

27. Dig this

29. Tuns

30. "— pin, pick …"

31. Midi department

32. Prince Valiant's son

33. Classifieds

35. Montparnasse pear

36. Manipulate

39. Top-notch

41. Signs up

43. Guarantee

44. *Nachtmusik* article

46. Moral system

47. "… after they've seen —"

48. Adhere to

49. Miss equivalent?

50. Witticisms

51. Marine starter

52. Lifter's move

53. Forwarded

56. "The most feeble thing in nature" (Pascal)

by Matt Gaffney

ACROSS

1. Has in mind
6. Letterman's ex?
9. Sad sack
13. Express, as a thought
14. Dutch painter Aelbert
16. Kazakh/Uzbek waterway
17. Allentown's favorite son
19. Blowout
20. One way to pay
21. Venerable ones
23. Lamp lighter: abbr.
24. Ingratiate
27. Come down with
28. Meth.
29. Algonquian tongue
30. Unknown
32. Lacks permission to
33. Well-founded substance?
34. *Across Spoon River* subject
39. Slowly sip
40. Goes it alone
41. Meadowlike
43. 1982 sci-fi film
44. Topeka clock zone
47. Man of Dadaism
48. Raises one's spirits?
50. Explorer De —
51. Cashew trees
53. Squire
55. Alice's coworker
56. Appomattox figure
59. Basic: abbr.
60. Elmo : Tarzan :: — : Jane
61. Baby's feeding time, maybe
62. Concrete foundation
63. Hellenized Aurora
64. Job enticements

DOWN

1. Sacred things
2. Without subterfuge
3. Heaters
4. Seminal computer acronym
5. 16-Across and others
6. Pvt., e.g.
7. Houlihan's Stadium player, for short
8. Vicious thing?
9. Carry on
10. North-ern exposure?
11. Problem for a *matelot*
12. Forcefully strikes
15. Song for Apollo

Solution is on page 235

18. Crawford or Ladd
22. Gains gradual acceptance with
25. Hawaii's state bird
26. Can't stand
29. Wouldn't mind
31. Fleischer and Hentoff
32. It's served every day
34. Monograms, as a bracelet
35. Energizer rival
36. Neutral zone
37. Cartoonist Drucker
38. "I'm —" (Beatles song)
42. "— nobody till somebody …"
44. Beach tote, maybe
45. Perform a '70s prank
46. Pole's adornments
49. Together
50. To-do
52. Lintel neighbor
54. Supremes cry
57. Profile
58. Grimley and Bradley

by William Marshall

ACROSS

1. Catches
5. Head piece?
10. Goes (for)
14. Essayist's sobriquet
15. Highland games pole
16. Post
17. Premeditated pace
20. Liner route
21. Columns for a 43-Across
22. Lincoln debater Douglas
26. Ancient Mexican
30. Adjutants
31. Fatimid
32. Educate
33. Somme-r time
36. Make whole
37. Three-time World Cup Alpine champ
38. Glaze base
39. Outcome
40. Eastern Church toppers, usually
41. Goddess of the hunt
42. Hawk's home
43. Stately gateway
44. It'll never fly
48. Too-too
49. Filled to the gills
54. Evolving customs
58. Lemonheads singer Dando
59. Violin precursor
60. Judgment
61. Blood-related prefix
62. Durable wood
63. Old European measures

DOWN

1. Pallets
2. Nautical position
3. Southwestern "monster"
4. Spinnaker or spanker
5. Like the Grand Canyon
6. Galley symbol
7. Desert wear
8. Tennis term
9. Grand — (*Evangeline* setting)
10. Muscat natives
11. Elbows on the table?
12. Saturn satellite
13. Winter fall
18. Farm machine
19. Jean of "Make Room for Daddy"
23. North Carolinian
24. Yarn spinners
25. Warhol's Sedgwick
26. Unexciting
27. Straw in the wind
28. Impart
29. Make hay while the sun shines

Solution is on page 235

32. Dravidian language
33. Part of QED
34. A Sinatra
35. Catchall phrase
37. Unit of metrical time
38. Douglas, for one
40. Exclude
41. Kind of tire
42. Glandular prefix
43. Course of action
44. Crescents
45. *Ancien* — (alumnus)
46. In conflict
47. Poet Nash
50. Current event?
51. Impress, as leather
52. Chemical compound
53. Mil. awards
55. Past *due*
56. Jewish title of respect
57. — system (blood-typing determinant)

SUITED TO THEIR JOBS

by Xan Lattimore

ACROSS

1. Filmdom's Tamiroff
5. Characters in a Boulle novel
9. Part of an agora
13. Chemical prefix
14. Computer list
15. Shrub shoot
16. Pool hustler?
18. Daryl Hannah role
19. Band instrument
20. Pad
22. Low-fat label word
23. Romantic piano piece
24. Tex-Mex item
27. Rent from a renter
28. Takes home
29. Craftiness
30. Was afflicted with
33. "Make my day," for one
34. Choice seat setting
35. Visibility problem
36. Former JFK visitor
37. Champagne quantity
38. Open discussion
39. Camden Yards player
41. Words on certain footwear
42. Early cinema offerings
44. Avian features
45. Smart
46. Fountain option
50. Govt. revenuers
51. Ragtime composer?
53. Anne Nichols character
54. Intent
55. As anticipated
56. Karachi's region
57. "Permit me"
58. Comice, e.g.

DOWN

1. Combine: abbr.
2. The good Eartha
3. Bring — (make conform)
4. Contracts of a sort
5. Love, in Liguria
6. Teller's partner
7. See 54-Across
8. Apt
9. Where to find the groom
10. Hairstylist?
11. Bribed
12. Type size
13. "I — lineman for …"
17. Whit
21. Everybody in Berlin?

Solution is on page 235

23. Assembled

24. See 50-Across

25. Some batteries

26. Ringmaster?

27. "If You Knew —"

29. 47-Down's lack

31. Sky blue, to Pompidou

32. Short sample

34. Aphorism

35. Drives exceptionally well?

37. Wrath, envy, etc.

38. Dick Tracy foe

40. Controlled (with "in")

41. Evelyn's brother

42. Some *madrileñas*: abbr.

43. Feet, to Ovid

44. Garlic sauce

46. 6/6/44

47. Killer whale

48. Forbidding

49. Wonder

52. Mauna —

by Alex Vaughn

ACROSS

1. Bout enders
5. Reeves/Bullock film
10. Cause of ruin
14. Concerning
15. Words before lunch
16. Above, in Aachen
17. Ibsen lady
18. Fiddling boatman?
20. Gloaming
22. Needlework of a sort
23. Bubblehead
24. Away
25. In
27. Adversity
31. Dockside hoist
32. Goodman's stompin' site?
33. Violinist Bull
34. Camp sights
35. Moisten
36. 23-Across, in the U.K.
37. Legendary predator
38. Deli roll
39. Show dread
40. Orbit's farthest point from the sun
42. Happy tabby
43. Expletive in the comics
44. K
45. Exonerates
48. Guidebook
51. Senate boatman?
53. Proofreader's mark
54. Pay to play
55. — a time
56. Mall habitué
57. 8th-cent. invader
58. Paloma's dad
59. Toast topper

DOWN

1. Cast
2. Be cognizant
3. Senate boatman?
4. Pacific coast yawpers
5. Dapper, in Dieppe
6. Arrogantly obtrusive
7. Vermont, to its neighbor au nord
8. H
9. The Waterworks author
10. Utah sights
11. Be on the lookout?
12. Tyrant of 60 A.D.
13. Cube-ist Rubik
19. Dennis of films
21. "Whosoever liveth and believeth — …"
24. Auctioneer's implement

Solution is on page 236

25. Gulf of Guinea seaport
26. Jamboree attendee
27. Former Rams QB Pat
28. *Show Boat*-man?
29. Start of a '52 slogan
30. Gospel fisherman

32. Other Utah sights
35. Marina shack
36. "My heart is — stone" (*Othello*)
38. Brassy honk
39. Campus area
41. Rubber rubber
42. Magician's word
44. — Abdel Nasser

45. Ellington's "— Blues"
46. Late-night host
47. — *perpetua* (Idaho's motto)
48. Small swelling
49. Appomattox signature segment
50. City on the Truckee
52. Bambi's aunt

by Brendan Emmett Quigley

ACROSS

1. Feather's branch
5. Note-able Khan?
10. Latch onto
14. Nuncupative
15. Badger kin
16. Sign of things to come
17. Quadri-, doubled
18. Awe-inspiring
20. Seuss classic
22. Buried
23. Kobe currency
24. Scholasticism founder
28. Conductor Koussevitzky
30. G.W.'s gp.
33. Card count, in Nero's deck
34. It may be civil
36. Haberdashery purchases
40. Barrett Strong hit
44. Dissipate
45. "— sing you to sleep, after …"
46. Kohl's country: abbr.
47. Elevs.
49. A little night music?
53. Jockey Eddie
57. — *War* (book by 60-Across)
59. Coffee pref.
60. See 57-Across
64. Goodman's genre
67. Jewelry setting
68. Cabbagelike plant
69. Think out loud
70. Offspring of: suffix
71. Canned
72. Rhyme or reason
73. 1987 Costner role

DOWN

1. Stands on the midway
2. Ring champ Moore
3. Not for minors
4. Coalition
5. Mediterranean vacation spot
6. Feeding, as a foal
7. Egyptian deity
8. Pocketed
9. "Yo!" from Ho
10. Stovepipes
11. French compadre
12. He's a real doll
13. Cotswolds country: abbr.
19. Write
21. *"Sí sí!"* at sea
25. Lamb, another way
26. Mortgage, e.g.
27. Atomizer emanation
29. Broadway's Lola
31. Start

Solution is on page 236

32. Mass seating

35. Breathing specialists: abbr.

37. Communes (with)

38. Newsstands

39. Abby, to Ann

40. Bucks beginner

41. Ancient history

42. Certain cop

43. Trapdoor

48. Besmirches

50. Decorative

51. Vandellas' lead singer

52. Way out

54. Bearded

55. Outfit

56. Actor Edward James

58. Run the show

61. Actress Velez

62. "The doctor —" ("Peanuts" notice)

63. Improvised weapon, maybe

64. Jamaican sound

65. Wicked stuff?

66. Land in the Seine

by Jeane Vesper

ACROSS

1. Joe Penny role
5. Unionist Chavez
10. Obsessed seaman
14. Take off
15. "— no questions …"
16. P-QB4, e.g.
17. Pierce portrayer
18. Base maneuver
19. Well-financed gp.?
20. Strange
21. "DON'T GO"
23. Gods' venous fluid
25. Overrun
26. *Shane* star
28. Military hub
33. Cagney character
34. Relief pitcher's stats
35. Mom's *hermano*
36. Demon barber of Fleet Street
37. Tensed (up)
38. Knucklehead
39. Hamlisch show tune
40. Hawaiian dwellings
41. Bring into being
42. Intensify
44. Holy city?
45. Having a two-letter monogram: abbr.
46. Condiment container
47. SPEAK CIRCUITOUSLY
52. *The* — (Uris novel)
55. Vishnu incarnation
56. Bucks
57. Waiter's handout
58. "This — outrage!"
59. Auto-purchase alternative
60. It may be cast
61. Knit
62. Trencherman
63. U2 singer

DOWN

1. Playwright Anouilh
2. Wheel bar
3. SHARED A FEW LAUGHS
4. LAX datum
5. Half of the Dioscuri
6. To be: Sp.
7. Set aslant
8. Asian nurse
9. Drew differently
10. Microscope sight
11. Kachina worshiper
12. *Pas sans*
13. Call's mate
21. Eschew
22. Film settings
24. Habré's country

Solution is on page 236

26. Man of many parts?
27. TV biggie Arledge
28. Endorser
29. Thresholds
30. BECOME STEADIES
31. Squelched, as a squeak
32. "— worry"
34. Convince
37. Kyser's Ish
38. Proofer's mark
40. Actor Cronyn
41. Spell
43. Available
44. NYSE figure
46. Hunt
47. Top of the tumbler
48. Cushion
49. Fed
50. Nitrogenous compound
51. Commuter's hope
53. Mystery writer?
54. — and the Paycock
57. Taw's kin

by Henry Hook

ACROSS

1. — *My Father Told Me*
5. Diet aid
10. Terry cloth inscription
13. It takes a bow
15. Fred's sister
16. "He had hi-i-igh hopes ..."
17. Stevies
19. Sodium hydroxide
20. Type of suspicion
21. Meaningless
23. Inimical
24. Down on the map
25. Waylay
29. Skirt
32. Coloring agents?
33. "— Mrs. North"
34. Classical starter
35. Israeli port
36. U.S. Defense Secretary (1969–73)
37. Erode, in a way
38. The word?
39. Yellow and black humors
40. Desert
41. Keyboard feature
43. Suffused
44. More appealing
45. Little, in Lyons
46. Ashcan, e.g.
48. Ramose
53. Ingrid's daughter
54. Glenns
56. List shortener
57. Bacon bit?
58. — *couture*
59. Comic sound
60. Unwieldy pencils
61. Pre-Christmas purchase

DOWN

1. Some have riders
2. Mangle alternative
3. Crossword bird
4. Bicarb
5. Streisand role
6. "— Rock and Roll Music"
7. *Alouette* bill
8. Norwegian breed
9. Echo
10. Daryls
11. Death Valley county
12. Olla
14. "— in a Shadow"
18. Sumptuous
22. Overseas business abbr.
24. Rises majestically
25. *Watership Down* writer
26. "— Runneth Over"

Solution is on page 236

27. Shelleys

28. Actress Mary

29. Heath bush

30. Plunder, old-style

31. Made wailing noises

33. Cheeky?

36. Defamer

37. Understand

39. Agrees with

40. Start

42. AFL mate

43. Suffer

45. Victims

46. WWI German admiral

47. Summon

48. Prattle

49. Hammer part

50. "And eternity in an —" (Blake)

51. Are: Sp.

52. Like a basso profundo

55. Baton Rouge sch.

by Robert Wolfe

ACROSS

1. Ransack
6. Rework
11. Wane
14. Inaccuracy
15. Loon, e.g.
16. Exist
17. Oldest New Zealander
18. Soon to have a baby?
20. Teensy
22. Trident features
23. Labor leader Eugene
25. Glacial pinnacle
28. Sandy tract
29. Mickey's ex
30. Biked
32. Homily: abbr.
33. Formal statements
35. Bails
37. Acid neutralizers
40. Changed the surface of

44. Designer de la —
46. Habituate
47. Band of sparks
50. Race official
53. Vogue, in Vosges
54. Beak's base
56. Fragrant root
57. Aide: abbr.
58. Affirmatives
60. Bit of hose
62. Make great progress?
65. "— just one of those ..."
68. Brooklyn trailer
69. Photographer Dorothea
70. Belt
71. Roman bronze coin
72. Foils' cousins
73. Armor skirt

DOWN

1. Sleeper's phenomenon
2. Keogh kin
3. Since a long time ago?
4. Arboreal creature
5. Mavourneen's land
6. Redacted
7. Asbestos, e.g.
8. Stowe girl
9. Ship-shaped clock
10. "Confound it!"
11. Frankie and Cleo
12. Lorenzo's mom
13. Jet d'eau
19. 'Twixt or 'tween
21. Avail
23. Duchamp's movement
24. Sinister
26. Birdlike
27. Yield

Solution is on page 237

30. Appears to less advantage
31. Procrastinate
34. Salt
36. Japanese honorific
38. Involved with
39. Night light
41. Has effect on both sides?

42. Piccadilly statue
43. Former Yankee Bucky
45. Set up
47. Gum arabic
48. Far
49. Thick liqueurs
51. Shades
52. AK native
55. Chemical ending

57. Sicilian crater
59. Clearance
61. Item for Adrian Messenger?
63. Pool unit
64. Hamlisch hit
66. — *longa, vita brevis*
67. Marie *ou* Jeanne: abbr.

by Alex Vaughn

ACROSS

1. —-pie
5. Party with a capital P
9. Pop artist Oldenburg
14. Gets mileage out of
15. Look like a wolf?
16. Depend
17. Obtain
18. Intimate
19. Blast from the past
20. Herbalist's bioenergy measurement
23. Typical lead-in
24. First-rate
25. Reproach to Brutus
27. Pompeii overlay
28. First degrees, maybe
31. Like the old gray mare?
34. Will Rogers prop
36. Crumb
37. Herbalist's triumph over pain
41. Zee, by the Dee
42. Hire
43. Cameo stone
44. Linguist's suffix
45. Honorific on an env.
46. One from Dubrovnik
49. Glove sz.
50. Polar sight
54. How herbalists develop remedies
60. *Catch-22* star
61. "Must've been something —"
62. Bama's Bryant
63. Hagiology entry
64. *"Sacré —!"*
65. Swim-meet section
66. A and B?
67. Namby-pamby one
68. Living and dead

DOWN

1. Restraints
2. "While memory holds —" (*Hamlet*)
3. "— porridge hot …"
4. Those who dream
5. Witticism
6. Ex-Met Tommie
7. Bed brace
8. Marriage goddess
9. Chattanooga, for one
10. French textile center
11. "— Love Her'"
12. Sponsorship
13. Appear
21. Do-over, on the court
22. Chaliapin and Pinza
26. Pakistani leader Mohammad Zia —
27. Obstinate ones

Solution is on page 237

28. Godsend
29. —-bargy (squabble)
30. "Babe" singers
31. Confusion
32. Chemical suffixes
33. Person Friday
35. Loser to DDE
38. Milieus

39. Onetime Edison employee
40. Teddy-bearlike
47. Precinct house routine
48. HS seniors' exam
49. Title spot
51. Habitable
52. "There's — that I heard of …"

53. Combustible heaps
54. Whence the dawn
55. Penetrating portrayal?
56. Children do it
57. Barbecue favorite
58. Former Sudanese Republic
59. Tabloid tidbit

by Robert Wolfe

ACROSS

1. Settles (into)
6. Conclude
11. Cambridge coll.
14. Minos' realm
15. Actress/comedienne Anne
16. Hockey Hall of Famer
17. Sioux Nation member
18. Peach stone?
20. Famous conference site
22. *Platoon* director
23. Orwell's alma mater
25. Lofty prefixes
29. Fierce Olympian
30. With 65-Across, "Lady Love" singer
31. Seafood bit
33. Contrapuntal song
35. Mother, at times
40. Songs of lament
43. Alleviate
44. Catalysts
46. Square measures
47. What Ali did well?
50. Dijon donkey
51. San —, Italy
55. Startle
56. Once, once
57. It's set to go off
59. British yard
61. Lively dance?
65. See 30-Across
68. Broke bread
69. City on the Moselle
70. *Some Like* —
71. Part of HMS
72. "… for — broke loose in Georgia" (Benét)
73. Some museum pieces

DOWN

1. Habitat: prefix
2. Ramus
3. What saws do?
4. An Allen
5. Pinniped
6. Spear
7. Born
8. U.S. airspace regulator
9. Stat for 31-Down
10. Shafts
11. Dynamo
12. Papas of Greece
13. Kilmer work
19. Greek letter
21. Make an antimacassar
23. Bugs' pursuer
24. Peter O'—
26. Mil. flier unit
27. Gen. Bradley
28. Desiccated

Solution is on page 237

31. Former Toronto pitcher Dave

32. "Chill out!"

34. Mayonnaise maker

36. Apocrypha bk.

37. Sob?

38. Yanni's ex

39. Adjust

41. Chemical endings

42. Flight part

45. Yemana on "Barney Miller"

48. Ruth's output

49. Supplement

51. *Hollywood* — (bio of 53-Down)

52. Delight

53. Powerful movie tycoon

54. Dig it

56. Lyric Muse

58. The stuff of legend

60. Math branch

62. Before, to Blake

63. Baseball's Hodges

64. Slippery character

66. Mauna follower

67. What some stars signify: abbr.

by Ernie Furtado

ACROSS

1. Make a fresh start
6. Idol
10. Follower of Joel
14. Part of *"veni, vidi, vici"*
15. First name in mystery
16. Tree trunk
17. Second-stringer
18. Marlene's *Blue Angel* costar
19. Kin of etc.
20. Tumbler tumbler
21. Beknighted actor?
24. Genealogy sci.
25. Chemical suffix
26. Singer in a Dutch town?
31. Malign
36. "— That Dream" (1939 song)
37. Libau native
39. Linda or Biff
40. "Vaya Con —"
41. Chilling
43. Integument
44. Ex-Nugget Dan
46. Martin of "Hill Street Blues"
47. This, to Julio
48. Shadow spot
50. Comic bandleader?
52. Zoological foot
54. Thunder Bay prov.
55. Stony Gunn portrayer?
61. Mary's 40-Across duet partner
64. Balcony area
65. Hunter of fiction
66. Motionless
68. Movies' Mowbray
69. Fax
70. Spirits
71. Absolute
72. More than *un peu*
73. *Unsafe at Any Speed* author

DOWN

1. Imperil
2. — *homo*
3. Not a one
4. It'll never fly
5. Reticular
6. Milwaukee export
7. *Babes in* —
8. Equally
9. Stage producer Hayward
10. Genesis figure
11. Marquand creation
12. Norse patron saint
13. Reflexive pronoun
22. Fanon
23. Experience vertigo
24. Grimm character
26. — *and the Cruisers*
27. Kenyon or Miller
28. Notched, as leaves

Solution is on page 237

29. Submissive

30. Channel

32. Arden, for one

33. Mennonite offshoot

34. Devilfish

35. Give to

38. Stratum

42. He's the Rocket Man

45. Kisser's target

49. Abhor

51. Annapolis graduate

53. Cleave

55. Littleneck

56. Function

57. Temple's first

58. Allele

59. Windmill slat

60. Machiavellian justifier

61. Give, for now

62. Site of a Perry victory

63. The big house

67. School gp.

by Chuck Deodene

ACROSS

1. Sax-y type
5. Crockett and Tubbs' beat
10. Wide-eyed
14. Bard's sunrise
15. Respond to
16. Peignoir
17. *Quod — faciendum*
18. Arctic tourist's comment?
20. Vocation
22. Witticism
23. Atelier models, often
24. Result of jetliner overproduction?
26. Pt. of DNC
27. Mary's boss at WJM-TV
28. Some home improvement workers
31. Palindromic rockers
34. Motley
38. Tampico time piece
39. Andean stampede?
42. Wrinkly-faced pooch
43. Carolina river
44. Part of Robert's signature
45. Manatee
47. Youth
49. Harbor sight
50. WWII invasion planning?
56. Nickname for Walter Johnson
58. Leaf's main vein
59. Dredging substance
60. Sushi gourmand?
63. Tarzan portrayer Lincoln
64. Brooklet
65. Printing press part
66. Lashes
67. Take off
68. Of import
69. Role for Della

DOWN

1. Words of approval
2. Large-eyed lemur
3. Zealot's offering
4. Dodging apprehension
5. Red head
6. "And, behold, — quickly" (Revelation)
7. Dumas character
8. Zoo barriers
9. Roomy place?
10. Engaged in forensics
11. Prize for Popov
12. Haunting wind
13. Some old Chevys
19. One of Newton's primaries
21. Prefix meaning "outer"
25. Time to get home
28. With minimum risk

Solution is on page 238

29. Bother

30. Everything-must-go event

31. Hannibal's obstacle

32. Risqué

33. Short piano piece

35. 1/100 hectare

36. Evening student's aim, initially

37. Plumbing joint

40. Orbital point

41. *Enterprise* excitement

46. Curl up

48. Litter cry

50. Bagpipe pipe

51. Super Bowl XX winning coach

52. Red as —

53. "It's the truth!"

54. Prints, as computer data

55. Rubbish

56. Drudge of yore

57. *Waiting for God* author

61. Get-up-and-go

62. Mock or crock ender

by Norma Steinberg

ACROSS

1. Fit
5. Consider
9. Fashion line?
13. Composer Janácek
14. Sampler word
15. Capital of French Indochina
17. Out of air
18. Base
19. Big wind?
20. AY
22. Darts
23. Part of a key chain?
24. Isaac of music
25. Exterior
28. Sniffs one's nose (at)
30. Bactrians, e.g.
32. Argyll hat
33. Absurd

37. Fixed
39. Trappings
41. Caterpillar creation
42. Tugboat Annie, perhaps
44. Sipped slowly
45. Gets around
48. Town on the Thames
49. Fistfight
51. GI lullaby of a sort
53. Chills out
54. TREA
59. Natural dos
60. "… — star to steer her by"
61. First name in sopranos
62. *Chambre*
63. Influence
64. Coin collector?
65. Retinal cells

66. Appear
67. Muddle

DOWN

1. Opener for Romeo
2. It's a cinch
3. Install, as software
4. Spanish 1 verb form
5. Mating game
6. Humble homes
7. Illustrious
8. Unite
9. Holiday horn
10. EAR
11. 1973 Rolling Stones hit
12. Ditches
16. Connections
21. Cry uncle
24. Some pageant entrants
25. Notoriety

Solution is on page 238

26. Song from *Lilies of the Field*

27. OL

29. Hearing aid

30. Dude

31. Frame

34. Plus

35. Foreclosure document

36. Stripling

38. Role model for 36-Down

40. Company

43. Party

46. Maids of Fife

47. Arab's burden?

49. To date

50. Sophia's husband

52. Bible song

53. Spanish newspaper article

54. Spells (out)

55. Ill-considered

56. Onetime governor Grasso

57. 8th-cent. prophet

58. Newton's forte

by Alex Vaughn

ACROSS

1. Sweater letter
4. Kind of acquaintance?
8. Bowie's battleground
13. "Oh!" de Cologne
14. Where Mets meet
15. Togalike
16. Turk's pastel hat?
18. Booth, Drood, Newman
19. Farewell gesture
20. Poet Heaney
22. Staggered
24. Overly
25. Mornings
28. Sikh's sauna headwear?
32. Draftsmen, once?
35. "— she blows!"
36. Real or fourth
37. W. Coast academe
39. Explosive
41. "¡— bien!"
42. Rode an updraft
45. Atomic particles
48. Comic cry
49. Twain-inspired cap?
51. Rile
52. Greensboro-to-Raleigh dir.
53. Time to wear down
58. Alphas' antipodes
61. Positive-thinking man
62. Go "Brrrrrrr"
65. Scottish hatter's get-involved slogan?
67. Sovereign's surrogate
68. Adam's apple area?
69. First Burmese prime minister
70. Ape Tomlin's Ernestine
71. Saxophone, e.g.
72. ER staff

DOWN

1. — *Lion* (Plimpton)
2. All part of the act?
3. "— a dream" (King)
4. Most wheyfaced
5. Certain TV channels
6. Vintner's dregs
7. Stupor
8. Grueling
9. Precepts
10. Beekeeper's prefix
11. *12 Angry* —
12. GI uniforms
15. Strip of stripes
17. Pass between mountains
21. Bkg. convenience
23. Ecclesiastic deg.
25. Degrade
26. Dull finish
27. Tiptoe

Solution is on page 238

29. Take tiffin
30. Palmer, to pals
31. Hwy. or tpke.
32. Certain bar fare
33. Search in depth
34. Loose
38. Okla. neighbor
40. Crag
43. Lead or lawrencium
44. Forsake
46. Partner of improved
47. Allowance
50. Panhandle
54. Sch. lobby
55. Ryan's daughter
56. Kudu's cousin
57. Uncle of fiction
58. "— the river and through …"
59. The sun, for one
60. Aspect
62. Men of La Mancha: abbr.
63. Layer
64. "Down and down —"
66. Churchill's sign

by A.J. Santora

ACROSS

1. See 57-Down
7. Most shrewd
13. Curvetted
14. Did planting work
16. Fashion, in Paris
17. Casey Jones, e.g.
18. Throbs
20. "The X-Files" subj.
21. Symbolic gridiron prize
24. — *dansant*
25. Gabby of oaters
26. Ordinal ending
28. Plays for a fool
30. Khomeini lived there
31. Start of a quote about Cecil B. De Mille
33. Middle of the quote
36. End of the quote
38. Flap
41. *The Hostage* playwright
42. Gun gp.
43. Became a couple
45. Past *due*
46. Vicinity
48. Ozone
49. Japanese seaport
52. "— nine days old"
54. Forgo
58. Ezra's follower
59. Conceive
60. Duel attendee
61. Sierra Nevada pass

DOWN

1. "— things bright ..."
2. Mare
3. Robin's sitcom costar
4. Narrative verse
5. Names anew
6. Journalist St. Johns
7. Jargon
8. Desire
9. Famed Speaker
10. Lo-o-ong time
11. Ocarina
12. Baby's ring
14. "— of morn" (Keats)
15. Most shriveled
19. Kind of housekeeper
21. Military command ctr.
22. Sports org.
23. "— Car" (TV oldie)
27. Family of U.S. jurists

Solution is on page 238

28. Spree

29. Gray shade

31. Play — with (make trouble)

32. Molding tool

34. Home loan agcy.

35. Middle: abbr.

36. Secure

37. Showy African flowers

39. Unwinder's room

40. Army wear

43. Erstwhile emperor's title

44. Ascended

47. Prosaic

49. Fictional captain

50. "… hear — drop"

51. Prod

53. "— Ramsey"

55. Japanese honorific

56. An Amerind

57. With 1-Across, end of Kansas' motto

101 THINK POSITIVELY

by Randolph Ross

ACROSS

1. Tripe
8. Pragmatist
15. Galápagos country
16. West Indies nation
17. Start of a quote
19. Native of Belgrade
20. Classical starter
21. "Paper —" ('73 song)
22. Rigid
24. Baseball stats
27. Constructed: abbr.
30. War baby
32. NCOs
36. Sheeplike
38. Source of quote
40. Greenhouses
42. Sharon or Peres
43. Middle of the quote
45. Waterway
46. "— Tu"
47. Sometimes it's moving
49. H.S. group
50. Consumer concern
51. Diamonds' color
53. Beast's Beauty
57. Saving plan
59. 18-Down feature
63. End of the quote
67. Fission device
68. Scouting boat
69. Hemingway, in Madrid
70. Director Sturges

DOWN

1. Great tennis returns
2. Yearn
3. Sorry one
4. Zingers
5. Humorist George
6. Examine
7. Gaelic
8. Freudian concern
9. Robinson's title
10. Certain fruits
11. Chinese leader?
12. Energy measures
13. French thought
14. "Drive" group
18. Bellini opera
23. Reviewer Roger
25. Northern sea
26. Annoys
27. Lenny director
28. To have, in Paris
29. Part of a ship's hull
31. Midwestern Indians
32. Odette or Odile

Solution is on page 239

33. Highlanders

34. Flooring specialist

35. Moments of temper

37. Slangy negatives

39. Platitudinous

41. "Tell — the judge"

44. Bandleader Shaw

48. Expunger

50. Small change

52. British titles

53. Reveal

54. Peeping Tom

55. Bank transaction

56. Time/Life publisher

58. Invite request

60. *Norma Rae* director

61. Analogy words

62. Solar deity

64. Understood

65. NFL player

66. Cyprinoid fish

by Randall Hartman

ACROSS

1. Ho's "Yo!"
6. Uraei
10. Clearance
14. Asperse
15. Clannish sort?
16. Bound
17. Heretic's belief, maybe
18. Join closely
19. Style-setter Giorgio
20. Bermuda Triangle call
22. Most hard-line
24. Signs of stress
28. Start-up money
29. Ward-heeler's boss
30. Forbidding
32. Photographs
36. Two of a kind
38. Consumes
40. The end of —
41. Author of the novel hidden in this puzzle
44. Out of the way
45. Physiologist Pavlov
46. "Smooth Operator" singer
47. Late
49. *Das Rheingold* role
51. Eur. country
52. Elmo : Tarzan :: — : Jane
54. Plows, e.g.
56. Self-centeredness
60. Aldous Huxley's — *and Essence*
61. Screen, as eggs
62. Meet
64. Pickle
68. Sailor's stern
69. Sicilian resort
70. Chameleon cousin
71. Jardinieres
72. Brio
73. Rhyme or reason

DOWN

1. Earlobe
2. Pliant
3. Butterfly's sash
4. *Siddhartha* author
5. Light tan
6. Balaam's mount
7. Dresses down
8. Meter maids?
9. 1982 Best Actress
10. Positions
11. Leeds stream
12. 24 Hours of —
13. Censor, in a way
21. Guinness, e.g.
23. Played it again
24. Look
25. Rugged
26. Baseball class, e.g.

Solution is on page 239

27. Bar order

31. Ruff's mate

33. John Tesh's genre

34. NYSE figure

35. Ex-Bear Gale

37. Coupon clippers

39. With-it

42. Medicinal plant

43. It has a caste of thousands

48. Having a trace

50. Leaders of the pack

53. Artemis' counterpart

55. Spaghetti-western director Sergio

56. See 5-Down

57. Peek

58. *The Good Earth* wife

59. *Platia Syntagma* city

63. Cheerful word?

65. Parisian's style

66. Circus barkers

67. End of it

103 APPROPRIATELY PUT

by Matt Gaffney

ACROSS

1. Grass topper
4. Beat a dead horse, in a way
11. Presidential son
14. *Sí*, asea
15. Go into
16. Med. insurer
17. Make the point?
19. Riot
20. Loaded
21. Maestro Georg
23. Perplex
26. Stick in the mud
28. "Don't Bring Me Down" group
29. 1998 Olympic city
35. "By Jove!"
37. Embellish
39. Lavished attention
40. Calvary letters
41. Not taken in by
42. Loafer
43. Steals, old-style
44. "Am — best, or what?"
45. Words to live by
46. Mulder, for one
47. Mucho
48. Site of a 1905 uprising
50. Certain natural combination
51. Luke's work
53. Not quite dry
55. Escapes gradually
58. "Yeah, right!"
60. Guillaume's game
62. 1985 Zemeckis film?
67. Wimsey portrayer Carmichael
68. Montana's defense, once
69. Feller
70. '80s tough guy
71. Pearson and Lanin
72. Greek goddess of night

DOWN

1. One before U?
2. See here
3. Streisand album
4. Harmless
5. Muck-a-muck
6. Cilium
7. Dijon honey
8. Talks tricks
9. Ten, sounded out
10. Province
11. "You'll have it in a sec!"?
12. G.P.'s gp.
13. Kin of UNIX
18. It's worth more than *plata*
22. Fiddling with strings?
23. Wisconsin school
24. Hyundai model
25. Kayoed?
27. Set aside

Solution is on page 239

30. Supplement

31. Pierced

32. Pay one's dues

33. Ansers' cousins

34. *Golden Boy* dramatist

36. *Steamboat Willie* creator

38. Inflicts upon

49. Arch of Hadrian locale

52. Maestro George

54. Awe-ful sound

56. Sandusky's county

57. America West players

58. 18th-cent. Scottish philosopher

59. Way off yonder

60. Huck's rafting buddy

61. Piercing location

63. Offensive time?

64. *The Hundred Secret Senses* author

65. Moron lead-in

66. Jinx's spouse

by Bernice Gordon

ACROSS

1. Dumbo, for one
5. Flight part
10. Nichols hero
14. Table spread
15. Lustrous cloth
16. Gridder's gear
17. One earning a pretty penny?
19. Epithet for Tyson
20. *Dreamgirls* creator
21. Abet
23. Past *due*
24. "Shoo!"
26. Hunk
29. Ancient tribesman
30. Spare part?
33. Kyrgyzstan's — Mountains
34. Withdraw
35. Sign of success
36. Small finches
38. Sold for
40. Law, in Lourdes
41. Centaur slain by Hercules
43. Peerless
44. List ender
45. Spinning
46. Velez and namesakes
47. Gives voice to
49. Havergrass
50. Palma post office
52. Not-quite-perfect circle
56. Fougères friend
57. Parlor activity
60. 10-Across' love
61. Banks of baseball
62. Freshwater mussel
63. Shower gift, maybe
64. — *Entertainment!*
65. Weakens

DOWN

1. "The Virginian" star
2. Like a fine port?
3. *Ryan's Daughter* director
4. Pen's reservoir
5. Evil feeling
6. Negotiator's forte
7. Rocker DiFranco
8. Feminine suffix
9. Turncoats
10. Re certain combs
11. Setting for a quartet
12. Baal, e.g.
13. Feudal worker
18. Sea swallow
22. Large group piece
24. Part of BFA: abbr.
25. Looker
26. Actress Berry

Solution is on page 239

27. A k a Mary Ann Evans

28. Madge was one

29. Sir, in old Italian

31. Fabulous Castle

32. Serves as an augury

34. Music buff's purchase

37. Growing out

39. Circumspect

42. His, in Le Havre

46. *Symphonie espagnole* composer

48. Ipils and baobabs

49. Ancient Greek flasks

50. Fruity finish

51. Melville travel tale

52. Give out

53. — cloth (sheer fabric)

54. Impudent one

55. They're big in Hollywood

58. Royal letters

59. Literary miscellany

by Bernice Gordon

ACROSS

1. Exploit
5. Modern factory worker
10. Go around in circles
14. Asian border river
15. Head of Hollywood
16. Spread like butter
17. Frank Herbert classic
18. Germany, for Kohl
20. Clergy, nobility and bourgeoisie
22. Province of Cuba
23. Old Roman way
24. "Di Provenza il ——" (*La Traviata*)
25. Emperors
28. Muslim
32. Shady figure?
33. Procrastinator's word
35. Ducking appurtenance
36. First mate
38. Asors' kin
40. James of jazz
41. Supply new blood
43. Veranda
45. Turn left
46. Full of sand
48. "… days of —— doubt" (Raleigh)
50. Island in the stream
51. Letter opener
52. Old French taxis
56. Horns (in)
59. J. C. Harris character
61. Indian weight
62. Art Deco designer
63. Author of *Uhuru*
64. Elvis, e.g.
65. Explosive charge
66. Secretary of State, 1895–97
67. 100th of a rupee

DOWN

1. Filming technique
2. Feathered five-footers
3. Patrick Dennis novel
4. Halloween fare
5. Professional's recommendation
6. Some ladies' rooms
7. It's straight from the horse's mouth
8. Roman emperor in 69 A.D.
9. Calories, formerly
10. Stand
11. —— Bator
12. Cleft
13. Central point
19. Irani's money

Solution is on page 240

21. Short-necked duck
25. Brazilian state
26. Bark used for tanning
27. Panache
28. Greek Pax
29. 1982 Heston film
30. Greek vowels
31. Raptor's weapons
34. Prime time
37. In fetters
39. Ohio port city
42. *Bête* —
44. August 13, e.g.
47. — metal (variety of brass)
49. Milk-related
52. Nourishment
53. Obi box
54. Official deeds
55. Alone, in Avignon
56. Confine
57. North Carolina campus
58. Ancient mariner
60. "Half dust, half deity" (Byron)

by Sylvia Bursztyn

ACROSS

1. Spot check?
6. Palate, mouthwise
10. Mil. weapons
14. "Superchief" Reynolds
15. Sir Anthony Eden, for one
16. 1958 Pulitzer novelist
17. Said the bartender to the duck …
19. Dossier
20. Diminutive, in Dundee
21. Roasts instead of toasts
22. Common
24. Chow
25. James I's son
26. *Twelfth Night*, for one
29. Kiri Te Kanawa, e.g.
30. Pigmented eye part
31. A hole in the head
32. Have outstanding
35. Said the bartender to the sheep …
39. Know-how
40. Fred of early TV
41. Electromotive unit
42. Acolyte's milieu
43. Rivulets
45. Big-band singer Hilliard
48. Brigands' haven
49. Vigorish charger
50. Dynamic opening
51. — Na Na
54. Uptick
55. Said the bartender to the sparrow …
58. Lyrics of exaltation
59. Cairo river
60. Delete a PC file
61. It's for the birds
62. Robert of *The Dirty Dozen*
63. Thomas of Wales

DOWN

1. Rules of conduct
2. Old Persian kingdom
3. 1968 Plimpton portrayer
4. Lorna's dad
5. Gave a hand
6. Bridle fittings
7. Mudder's fodder
8. Scepter accompaniment
9. Elaborate
10. Tanzanian trek
11. "I want — just like …"
12. Scrimmage
13. Kiwi feature
18. Child's play
23. Merciless
24. Potluck, e.g.
25. Body of genuine works
26. Martí's homeland

Solution is on page 240

27. Through

28. Deliquesce

29. Sawyer's surface

31. Sound from Humpty Dumpty, maybe

32. Organ stop

33. Gait

34. See 24-Down

36. Jodie Foster, once

37. Undisclosed

38. By any chance

42. Nip in the bud

43. Golfer Middlecoff

44. Breached the peace

45. Cheboygan's lake

46. Notwithstanding

47. Stratagems

48. Dud

50. China setting?

51. Guarantee

52. "— real nowhere man …"

53. Symbol of Ra

56. Friends' pronoun

57. Ironic

1

```
G E T A . . S O D . . H O T T E A
A L E X . . I D A . . I N S E A M
L I M E S T O N E Q U A R R Y
A S P . . A U R A S . . P R O P S
. . . H Y P . . S P Y . . .
. . T A I . . . . A L A W
J O H N N Y A P P L E S E E D
O R A N G E F R E E S T A T E
B A N A N A R E P U B L I C S
. . T H O R . . . . . R E M
. . . N B A . . B O Y
S P A N O . . A G L O W . . Z O O
L E M O N A D E V E N D O R S
O L I V E R . . N O R . . E L A L
P E D A L S . . T V S . . M A N O
```

2

```
C L O P . . K I D D . . J O W L S
Z A N E . . E C R U . . O P R A H
E T T A . . L E A N . . S C A R Y
C H A L K L A T E C H I P S
H E P . . H E X . . B O U T
. . J A Y . . Y U M A . . S P A
I B S E N . . M A G E . . S W A P
T A K E S F O R G R A N I T E
C L I P . . A N D Y . . T I M E X
H E M . . P U S S . . H O P
. . T O N I . . J A M . . A S H
. . H A V E A G N E I S S D A Y
J O U S T . . N O E L . . P O M P
O W N E R . . O G R E . . O B O E
B E T T Y . . R O S Y . . T E A R
```

3

```
M D C C . . C H A P . . V I C A R
L E A H . . R O V E . . I G A V E
K I L O M E T E R S T O N E S
. . P E T E R . . P A R A D E
A B Y S M A L . . J I M . . D O N
P R O T O N . . M I D I . . A N T
T E R I . . R U B E N S . .
. D E C I L I T E R C A K E
. . K N O T T S . . L A B S
B E G . . F O E S . . L E E R A T
A L A . . L T S . . G E R M A N Y
S A L L I E . . G O N G S . .
K I L O G R A M F O O L I S H
E N O C H . . R E A R . . O V U M
D E P O T . . I N R E . . T Y P O
```

4

```
F U M E S . . B A L I . . N I L E
A P A R T . . I R O N . . I D O L
Y O U R O W N B U S I N E S S
E N D . . L E E S . . T E A S E
. . N E S T . . C A S T . .
O C T A N T . . M O S E Y E D
R H O S . . P E R I L . . N R A
G E T A L O A D O F F O N E S
Y E A . . I N S E T . . R U S E
. . P L A N E T S . . A R L I S S
. . L E S E . . O B E Y . .
P R I M O . . E T E S . . E P A
O U T O F S I G H T O U T O F
O L A N . . I S E E . . L A U R A
H E L D . . P A R R . . D R I E R
```

5

```
ACRE   BITT    THAT
TROY   ALOUD   SOME
TOTE   SERVO   ETON
UPST[AIR]SDOWNST[AIR]S
   EWE      EOS
 BREATHOFFRESH[AIR]
BOOTY  ALLOT   CEO
AMAH   CLEAR   FRAU
ABS    BOLOS   ALERT
LETSONESH[AIR]DOWN
   ETC      CIO
 ONTHELONEPR[AIR]IE
INAT   PAPAL   AIDA
RAIL   TRAIL   GEES
ANNE   ALLS    ERST
```

6

```
UMBRELLAS    BILES
POLEVAULT    UTILE
ALEXANDER    XEBEC
TIN   ELSE   OMEGA
RED USU ARM   RAN
ERECT  MAKE  TINT
EERIER  REC  HATS
    SPACERACE
DISC  CAT  PROMPT
INTO  KNOB  AKIRA
ASA EST RAM   SAY
REDID  ITOI   SNL
ICING  NEWMEXICO
ETUDE  ANNETYLER
SAMOS  SQUEEZERS
```

7

```
TIFF   POKES   OCHS
ETAL   AVIAN   OHOH
XCKENTETRAZZINI
THEDOORS   KEELER
     BIT  SEASIDE
STALLS  TOOL
EUBIE  BALI   FREE
XNESSEEWILLIAMS
YELP  MIND  ELVIS
   TINY   COMETO
HOPSING   SAX
ELAINE  ANTIGONE
XINGANDMAKINGUP
EVAN   CAPRI   ARIE
DAMS   EBSEN   TETE
```

8

```
CAREERS   SAWMILL
ONESDUE   TRAINEE
PISCINE   AIRSHOW
IMPUTED   PATHAND
LAID   COL    ALIE
OTTO  MOPED   PENS
TEESHIRT   RUSSET
    OMNIBUS
HERBIE   MANASSAS
OVER  STACK   PANT
MERE   ELK   ANDI
BROADEN   SPARTAN
REUTERS   TALKING
ESTHETE   ALDENTE
STEEPED   BEADIER
```

9

```
B E N I T O M U S S O L I N I
A M E R I C A N I N P A R I S
X M A S D E C O R A T I O N S
T E T   E A R   E K E   N E O
E T E   O N O S   I D E S
R T R E V   E A N   O O P S
    M E L A N G E   L U G E
G E N E R A L H O S P I T A L
A Y E R   M O O N S E T
Y E G G   P E R   S H O P S
    L E M S   A T A T   B A H
A M I   M H O   E V E   L I E
R E G U L A R E X E R C I S E
P R E S I D E N T R E A G A N
S L E E V E L E S S D R E S S
```

10

```
S P A R   R A T E   T H O L E
T A M E   O P E L   H O L E Y
A L E C   S A P S   E N D E D
B E N E F I C I A R Y   I D I
    D I N E D   A V E R S E
C A P E R   S T E V E
O U R   S H E B A T   A L A R
B R O N T E T I T L E N A M E
S A M E   R E D S E A   N I N
    U R G E S   R O D E O
H O L D I T   S H A N A
A U G   P O E T I C A F O R E
S T A M P   R E N T   I R O N
T O T I E   R E D O   S E M I
O N E O R   S P U R   H O E D
```

11

```
A B O V O   H U R T   R E D A
M I N E D   O V E R   O X E N
O Z O N E   S A N A   M E L T
    I S E E   O N T A R I O
M E A   S L A V   S U N T A N
A S T R A L   E M I T   S N Y
T E L A   O R A T O R
    I N M E D I A S R E S
    A U D I T S   I P S E
A R S   T I N A   A R N O L D
C U T L E T   S O M E   T Y S
C L A U D I A   C U B A
R I L L   O B I T   U L N A E
U N A L   N E N E   F A I N T
E G G S   S T E T   F I N I S
```

12

```
S O H O   V E N I   A L P S
C L E F   I T O R   L O U T
A L L F A S H I O N A B L E
B A M   S T E R N A   P R O
    S M E A R   S E E D I E R
S A M O A   S R I   R O T O R
R I A L T O   A D O R N
O M N I   V I C E S   J A R S
    E R O D E   T A U R U S
Z E B R A   E D S   S A M B A
A L L E G R O   H A N N A
P O E   E L A I N E   T W O
P A S S F O R V I R T U E S
E C H O   G O E S   O R A L
S H E D   Y O R E   Z E N O
```

13

```
S L E E P   M A T A   B A R T
C E L I A   O C H S   E C H O
O V E R T   T R E S   E C O N
T I M E I S H O N E Y   E N E
      N A P   S U P P E R
  S I N A T R A   S K I T
T I N E   I O U S   O S A G E
H A S T E N O T P A N T N O T
O M A H A   F O O L   I C E S
    T E S S   S T I L L E R
S O I R E E   L A O
N R A   L E S S I S A B O R E
A B B Y   S O N G   F A K I R
F I L E   A M A H   E D I N A
U T E S   W E P T   R E E D S
```

14

```
G A L A   S I N G   A M A Z E
A M O R   E R O O   D O M E S
S O F T H E A R T E D N E S S
P I T I E D   A H A   I N T O
      S I C E   I S N T
C O N T R A D I C T I O N
H U E S   S I N   P R I Z E
I Z E   R E T R I E S   V I M
P O D I A   E N G   Y E T I
  A C C O R D N O T I N I T
  E Y R A   S T E P
J A I L   E S S   I N P L A Y
O F T E N S H E D S T E A R S
A R O S E   E X I T   E P E E
N O R S E   R Y E S   S P A R
```

15

```
D E C   N A G   M A P   W A T
A T A T I M E   A B O L I S H
M A N A T E E   C E L E S T E
  T U R N S T H E O T H E R
G A I   O D E A   A F R O
O W N   N A S L   U N D
G L A M O U R S C H O O L
  E D N A   T A C O
  C L O T H E S M I N D E D
E M O   R O S A   H E Y
M O R T   C H I C   U K E
M O D E L B E H A V I O R
E L I S I O N   B A V A R I A
T A T T L E D   I N I T I A L
S H E   I R S   T A C   E M P
```

16

```
J A N E T   B A D E   A N X
A D A N O   W A D E D   C O Y
M A N S A R I B A L D   C B S
  M A N S A R A K E   B E E T
  A T T Y   T R O L L S
S P A R S E   B R E E Z E
P O P E   S A L A D F O R K S
A M P   M A N   A C E
S P E E D L I M I T   S T A T
  A N Y O N E   U T T E R S
C H R I S T   S T O A
L O A D   I S N A T U R E S
Y O N   S O L E M I S T A K E
D E C   A N A X E   L E V I N
E Y E   M S G T   E D E N S
```

17

```
B A L E _ N O E L S _ _ A D A M
F L U X _ C A R E W _ _ L O N I
L O C O M O T I V E _ _ B U N K
A N I T A _ S K I D _ _ A G E E
T E D I U M _ _ T E A C H _ _ _
_ _ C R A G G Y _ _ S O N A R
O T B _ A J A R _ S P R U C E
K A R A _ O P A R T _ E T N A
A M I N O R _ P O O L _ S E P
Y E C C H _ T H E M O B _ _
_ K E I T H _ P R O M P T
E B B S _ A W E D _ C R A S H
T O A T _ M A D A G A S C A R
T O T O _ P R I Z E _ H A L O
U S S R _ S T E E L _ T O M B
```

18

```
J A M B _ C Z A R S _ A C E S
O R E L _ L A L A W _ R A R E
T U T U _ E G O C E N T R I C
A M O E B A _ T E A T I M E S
_ _ M E N S _ T H E E _
_ D O S _ I N G E _ L O S
O L I V E R G O L D S M I T H
M A R I E A N T O I N E T T E
I N T E M P E R A T E N E S S
T A Y _ S T E T _ E D S
_ H A S H _ S I Z E _
A N A P A E S T _ R E L O A D
C A R A M E L I Z E _ I N F O
I R R S _ T O K E N _ A Z O N
D A Y S _ S W I N E _ N E X T
```

19

```
G O T _ W E P T _ E X P O
O F O _ P O U R E R _ A V E R
A T M _ R E R E L E A S I N G
T H A N E _ O H E N R Y _
S E T T E _ P I P E R _ H A G
_ J O H N T E S H _ A S I D E
M A J _ S E A T O _ S A B O T
E C U A _ C N O T E _ W E L T
S K I P S _ I R O N E _ R E Y
T A C E T _ Z I L L I O N S
A L E _ P E A C E _ G R A C E
_ T A R T A N _ H O T E L
H I G H T A I L S I T _ I N A
E Q U I _ S O L E L Y _ O C T
S S T S _ N Y S E _ N E E
```

20

```
V C R _ F O G Y _ A F R A M E
A L E _ L A R A _ R A I D E R
L I F E O F E M I S S Z O L A
E C L I P S E _ G E T Z _
T H E N _ N O O N _ O R F F
S E X _ C A B A R E T _ O I L
_ R A D A R _ R A L L Y
S M I S S Y S P E O P L E
C O U P E _ M E R I T _
O F F _ D A M A G E S _ M A L
W A F T _ P A N G _ J E T E
_ W H E Y _ Y O U K N O W
T H R E E M I S S I S L A N D
A M O E B A _ M U S E _ C A L
G O T T E N _ L E E R _ E L Y
```

21

```
D A C H A ■ A P P A L ■ W A S
E Y R E S ■ L O R N E ■ A V A
A N E X C E L L E N T ■ R I B
■ D O O R ■ E V A N E S A R
C R E S T E D ■ I S O L A T E
A O N E ■ M A N N ■ E W E S
M I Z ■ T I N A ■ S A G ■
P L A C E T O S T U D Y T H E
■ A X E ■ A R C S ■ W A R
T A L C ■ F L I C ■ K I W I
A M A T E U R ■ S U S A N N A
H A B I T S O F ■ M M L I ■
I Z E ■ H U M A N B E I N G S
T E L ■ O R A R E ■ A N G E R
I D S ■ S Y N O D ■ R E S T S
```

22

```
F I S H ■ D O F F ■ S W O O P
I D E A ■ E V I L ■ C A N D O
F I L L ■ B A J A ■ E X U D E
T O M F O O L I S H N E S S
Y M A ■ I N S ■ H E I R ■
■ A L E ■ A C D C ■ M A P
C R A N E ■ E G A D ■ G O B I
R O G E R O V E R A N D O U T
A V O W ■ V E N D ■ E A R T H
B E G ■ F O N T ■ I V Y ■
■ T R I M ■ A N E ■ M A C
F I V E D O L L A R B I L L
M O R S E ■ N A I F ■ E T T A
G O M E Z ■ E R G O ■ C Z A R
S T A T E ■ Y A N G ■ K I R K
```

23

```
B A S H ■ W E L D ■ A C I D
A T T U ■ M E D E A ■ N O V A
N E A T ■ E A S E S ■ G L E N
J A Y S I L V E R H E E L S
O M S ■ N O E L ■ E L L E ■
■ F A D ■ E R A ■ C A W
C A R N I V A L ■ L A T C H
D O L E ■ C O S B Y ■ T O R Y
E M C E E ■ T H E O D O R E
N A H ■ V E E ■ G A M
■ E M I L ■ A L U M ■ I S H
S M I L E Y B U R N E T T E
S O I L ■ V I N G T ■ T A R A
R O S A ■ E P E E S ■ C L I P
A T T N ■ N E R D ■ H Y P O
```

24

```
■ P I L E ■ O P E R A ■ A M P
■ E N O S ■ N A V A L ■ R A H
D R A W T H E L I N E ■ E R E
R U S ■ H E E L S ■ A A A
S K E T C H Y ■ F A C T S
E C H O ■ E E L ■ A L O H A
■ E N L ■ R E L I E D O N
G O O F F O N A T A N G E N T
E X P R E S S O ■ S T E
T Y P O S ■ A F C ■ E N D S
S M O G S ■ H A D D O C K
L O N ■ C O R A L ■ M O I
O R E ■ M A K E S A P O I N T
S O N ■ A G R E E ■ A N N E
T N T ■ D E A L S ■ L E O S
```

25

```
D E S P E R A D O   G O T A T
A C T I V A T E D   I N O N E
W H E N I D E A S   G I L D A
D O N   L I A R   G O N E R S
L E O N   O R S E L L   R E P
E D S E L     R I O   A T O
    L A C   O A T   O T T O
F A I L W O R D S C O M E I N
I N N S   W O E   H A N
R A F   A P T     R I S E S
E L L   B E C A L M   A C T A
H E A D O N   G O A S   O U T
O C T A D   V E R Y H A N D Y
S T E V E   A N N O U N C E R
E S S E S   S T E R N N E S S
```

26

```
C E S   I P A S S   S A M O A
A N I   T O R T E   P L A I T
E S E   C L E A R   A I S L E
S I C K H E A D A C H E S
A L L O Y     P E N N A N T
R E E S   T I T H E   A G U E
    O A T H   I T E M S
T R A N S I T I V E V E R B S
H A V E S   R E V E
A N E W   F U D G E   L A D D
W I N S T O N   V E N U E
  G L O R I A S T E I N E M
S P E E D   S M E A R   U N A
N O R A D   O M E N S   A N N
R I S K Y   N O R S E   L A D
```

27

```
E T T A   M I C E   H A R E M
L O R N   E C H O   A N A M E
A T A N   D A R N   R E D A N
B A N I   U N I   P L A I N T
O L S E N S   S K I   R O C A
R A P   E A S T E R   T I L
A B L E S E A M E N   R E P P
T S A R S   G A P   P O L A R
E T N A   H E S I T A T E T O
D I T   E L I T E S   S I C
E N A S   A Y S   R O S C O E
T E T H E R   L A M   C O N S
A N I O N   T A X I   A P I S
I C O N O   A N E T   L E S E
L E N E S   I D L E   P S T S
```

28

```
A R F S   A B O W   P R I M P
D O I T   H A R I   E E R I E
A(MAN)F O R A L L S E A S O N S
M O O R E   L E E R   E N D O
    M O N O   R O I L
O D A Y   C O M(MAN)D M E N T S
C E N   O O N A   E N C O R E
C O D E R   S T A   O T T E R
U R A N I A   E T A T   E N G
R O(MAN)H O L I D A Y   E S T E
    A N I L   N E A L
C L A N   E L E C   D A V I D
R O(MAN)C I N G T H E S T O N E
A L D E R   E N O W   O L G A
B L A D E   T A R E   R E E D
```

29

```
A I D A N D A B E T ■ A P O D
S T A T I O N A R Y ■ R O V E
L A M E N T A B L E ■ A L E X
O D A ■ E E R I E ■ F L I R T
P A G E R ■ C E S T A ■ S H E
E Y E S ■ P H D ■ R I C H E R
■ C A L I ■ H U R L E R S
■ S C A R E S ■ A S T A R E
S N I P E A T ■ I T O R
L I N E N S ■ P R Y ■ E S S E
A P E ■ A E S O P ■ O T T E R
S P A T S ■ P R I A M ■ R I N
H E S A ■ L I T E R A L I Z E
E T T U ■ E L E C T R O D E S
D Y E S ■ S T R E S S T E S T
```

30

```
C H A W ■ T H A W ■ C O C K Y
M Y N A ■ R O S E ■ O Z O N E
O P T I C A L A L L U S I O N
N E E S O N ■ P S I S ■ L B S
■ T E S S ■ H A T H
S M U ■ D A N G ■ M E E T M E
L I N K ■ C O O T ■ A R I E L
O L F A C T O R Y O U T L E T
B L I N I ■ D E P P ■ Z E N O
S E X I S M ■ S E E N ■ S Y N
■ N C O S ■ S N A P
A F T ■ O N E I ■ F R A C A S
B L O C K A N D T A C T I L E
L A N A I ■ A L E C ■ C A P E
E M E N D ■ T Y N E ■ H O O K
```

31

```
■ T O P S T A T U S
■ M I S S I S S I P P I
■ S E N S E L E S S N E S S
R E N ■ A U K ■ H E A R T S
A G U A ■ D E G S ■ X R A Y S
N E D D A ■ N O H I T ■ E L S
T R O O P S ■ O U R ■ A L E
■ R E O R D E R E D
V A N ■ H O G ■ S N A K E S
A I D ■ S O L O S ■ D I N G O
S T O I C ■ E D I T ■ R I G A
K A R N A K ■ B R A ■ F O R
L E S L I E N I E L S E N
R E A D D R E S S E S
T E D D A N S O N
```

32

```
A G R A ■ A B E L ■ T A B L E
L O O N ■ N O T E ■ O G R E S
S L A T ■ I N T O ■ W E A N S
O F M E I S S E N M E N ■
■ N E A ■ O R T E G A
P A C E D ■ I B I D ■ N O N
A C A D I A ■ A L I ■ A R A T
T H E G A P E S O F W R A T H
R I S E ■ H O I ■ Y I P P E E
I N A ■ I N C A ■ D A T E R
A G R E E D ■ L E O ■
■ E A S T O F S W E D E N
S P A R S ■ E A R S ■ R A M A
A R N I E ■ R H E A ■ I R I S
M O D E L ■ R U D Y ■ C E L T
```

33

```
B O A R . . S T O W . . . Z I P
O L P E S . T I E R . S E M I
Z I P P Y Z E B R A . C L A P
O V E R C A M E . S T O O G E
. A L I E N . R E S E N T E D
. . S E A M . M E R C Y .
R A Z E . N A M E . R E P E L
I D O . Z A M A R R A . I L E
P O O P O . I N G E . T A M E
. . P E N C E . E S T A .
R E H E A R S E . E R I C A
A B O L L A . R E D O L E N T
S O B E . Z E N D A V E S T A
P A I D . E R I E . E N T E R
S T A . S E E N . . D A D E
```

34

```
A L E R T . A B B A . A W A Y
C E L I A . L E A R . B A M A
C O M P U T E R T R A C K E R
. E R E C T . A D D E N D
C H A R O N . D Y E .
R A N . G A S P E . S T E A K
A R O O . N E O N . T A M P A
B L I N D T R I O M E M B E R
B A N C O . A S T I . P O L A
E N T E R . P E E L S . S E T
. S U E . D E I S T S
A S Y L U M . F I E N D .
S T E A M B O A T W I L L I E
C A L K . E D D A . L E E R Y
H Y P E . R E E L . E R A S E
```

35

```
S P A T . S I G M A . M O B
A L D A . A D H O C . S O L O
L A M B . D E E R H O U N D S
. T I L L . A T E . R I O T S
C E R E A L . T A S K . L I E
A A A . D I M O U T . M O M S
B U L L D O G S . O S A G E
. P E N S . D O U R
. H E N R I . B U G B E A R S
Y A M S . Z E R O E S . M A O
A L P . N E M O . S E L E C T
C L E A N . B M W . T I R E
H O R S E F L I E S . K I W I
T W O S . R E D I D . E G A D
S S R . O M E N S . S O Y A
```

36

```
S P I L E . S P A N . O N C E
T E L E X . H A R T . S E A T
A S L E E P A T T H E S W C H
N O E R R O R S . C A S T A
. C O P Y C A T . Y I N
A S S A I L . A L O P
T O O T S . W I D E . A S S T
I F T H E S H O E F S W E A R
P A S O . P I N T . O N T H E
. S H U N . L U S H L Y
R E B . O N E P A I R .
E Q U A L . S L A P S H O T
N U T T Y A S A F R U C A K E
K I T E . D E L I . S A T I N
O P E N . D A M E . S T E E D
```

37

```
S P A R E R I B S ■ ■ C H A P
A R M A D I L L O ■ S H A P E
S U M M O N S E S ■ T A M P A
S N A P ■ G A D ■ P R I M L Y
■ E N A T E S ■ S O I R E E ■
■ ■ G A R ■ D I S P E R S E ■
P A G E R ■ T I L E ■ D I E T
E N A ■ P E R V A D E ■ N E T
A T M S ■ S U E S ■ M A G D A
S E M E S T E R ■ S I C ■ ■ ■
■ C A T H E R ■ F U L C R A ■
B E R T I E ■ F U M ■ E I R E
A D A L E ■ C O M M E N T E D
K E Y E D ■ F R E E S T A T E
U S S R ■ ■ A D D R E S S E S
```

38

```
A S A P ■ L E A P S ■ ■ I P S O
B A R R ■ E L L I E ■ ■ N A T E
A L A E ■ S L O P E ■ T S A R ■
C O R S E T S U P P O R T ■ ■ ■
U M A S S ■ ■ ■ A S P I R E S ■
S E T ■ S A I L ■ ■ A G A P E ■
■ ■ S E N S E O F H U M O R ■ ■
■ T S E ■ T I T L E ■ E I S ■ ■
P I T C H I N G A R M S ■ ■ ■ ■
O R A T E ■ O F N O ■ O E D ■ ■
R E G A L I A ■ ■ M A R L O ■ ■
■ G R I D F O R M A T I O N ■ ■
D R E I ■ A T R I A ■ T O P E ■
O T R A ■ R E A D S ■ A L E E ■
A S S N ■ E R N S T ■ R E D S ■
```

39

```
S M U R F ■ O P E C ■ C R A B
A I M E E ■ R U T H ■ C U R E
T R A V E L I N C I R C L E S
■ ■ S L E E K ■ M A X I N E ■
F D A ■ F A N ■ D E N ■ N A T
L O R D O F T H E R I N G S ■
O R N E R Y ■ A B A T E ■ ■ ■
P E E R ■ ■ A R T ■ H I E D ■
■ ■ E V A N S ■ T H R O N E ■
■ M A K E S T H E R O U N D S
S Y M ■ R P I ■ L E G ■ A S K
A G A S S I ■ S T A N K ■ ■ ■
D O L L A R S T O D O N U T S
A S I A ■ I T E R ■ S E P I A
T H E W ■ N E M O ■ E W I N G
```

40

```
I N I G O J O N E S ■ A L A R
N A T U R A L I S T ■ S A N E
S T A T E M E N T S ■ S K I D
O I L ■ B A N E ■ I T E M S ■
L O I S ■ N I S A N ■ E A T ■
E N C E ■ O D E ■ S P A R T A
■ ■ D U D E S ■ L A Z I E R ■
S H E A R E R ■ P E R T E S T
T E N N I S ■ C R E T E ■ ■ ■
P A S S A S ■ O O P ■ C R A M
E T H ■ H A S N T ■ S E T A ■
T E R N S ■ E N O W ■ C A N ■
E D I E ■ B I O C H E M I S T
R U N E ■ A N T O I N E T T E
S P E D ■ R E E L T O R E E L
```

41

```
R O D E   S L I D E   C H E T
A H A B   H E N I E   O A T H
L A W B R E A K E R   U N T O
P R E S E R V E D   O R D E R
H E S   N E E D   M A T
      E E N   R E T R E A T
T A U P E   D I S S O L V E
A C R E   F L I P S   O L I N
R E S T O R E D   A M A S S
T R A I L E D   F A T
    T E E   F L U E   I R E
B A N J O   R O A D S I D E S
A L O U   K E Y W I T N E S S
B E A R   A B E E T   T A T E
A S H Y   Y A R D S   O L E S
```

42

```
P S I   A D S   A S P   N A M
U N D   T R I   P O O   A V A
B O O B O O S   P R O P M A N
  O L Y M P I C A T H L E T E
O P I E   A L A   A T A T
F E Z   H U E S   S C A R S
F R E D A S T A I R E E G
    A B E T   M I T T
  P R I D E F U L H O R S E
D E A L T   A P E S   O P T
A T I E   E L I   A M A H
C O N N I V I N G W O M A N
R I T E S O F   H O M I N I D
O L E   E K E   A J A   C E O
N E D   E E R   T O R   E L M
```

43

```
P O L S   S W I G   S I F T
A B U T   T O N I   A N I O N
S I M O L E O N S   L A V E R
S T E W A R D S   D U R E S S
E S T A T E S   T U T U S
    W H O   S W E E T P E A
P I C A S   S U I T S   O R E
O B E Y   F A R G O   S T A R
P E N   E A V E S   G A S S Y
E X T E N D E R   G U N
    U R G E D   H O L D T H E
M O R R I S   R E L A T I O N
A R I A N   H A L F G R A N D
I R E N E   B I L E   A R E A
  S S T S   O D O R   P A D S
```

44

```
A B A C I   M E S A   E L B A
T E X A S   O N U S   T A L L
V E E R S   P A S T   T O U T
S T L O U I S C H I N A S E A
    L E D   T I R O L
C H A I R E D     S P R I G
H O R N   A R U B A   D O N A
A S I A   L O R E N   N U L L
P E E P   S P U R T   A G E E
S A L O N   G I B L E T S
    L E A K Y   C E S
H C A E B M L A P S E I D N I
E A R P   M I Z E   T A R O C
N I N A   A N O N   L E A S E
S N O W   N E O N   E S T E S
```

45

```
A B C . M O D . . R E C A P
C U R B . E R R . O C T O P I
E M U L A T E A B R A H M A N
. S E A M . . W L S . M R S .
. . N O M I N A . A P E .
S T I C K Y S U B S T A N C E
A R G O . G N P . C O N D O S
R U N . G O O . G A I . I R S
A R O M A S . E E R . A N N A
H O M O P N O N E F O R G U Y
. . I O E . T I S S U E .
S O N . W R S . S N I T
C R I T I C A L P U T D O W N
O N E A L S . E E G . T W I N
T O S C A . . D A H . A T E
```

46

```
P L U S . P E W . T E A M
L A N C E . I D E A . R A N I
A N T I C . L I P S . U R I S
N E O . A B O T T I M E T L E
. . F R I T H . M A S H E R
T O M A T O . D O T .
A N E L E L O V E V A T O R
M I S S . R I M . I R A S
. T H E D A N C I N G D A R K
. A B E . O N E D A Y
A R M A D A . S A G A S .
T H E B A C K U S S R . B O W
L I D A . U N D O . L L A M A
A N A T . S E A N . S O L I D
S O L E . E N E . B I T E
```

47

```
M A C . B A M . P A S . H A P
A I L . L O O . A S K . O T O
P R O N O U N . S T E E R E R
. T I C T A C T O E M A R K
H A H N . O A R . E T R E
A R E . A Z A N . D R I E R
M C D O N A L D S L O G O
. C A R T . I O N E .
. S C I F I T V S E R I E S
L O T U S . A A S E . N A T
O R E L . S N L . A F R O
D I A T O N I C S C A L E
G O R S H I N . A L B E R T A
E L I . I D E . D U E . N O X
R E C . O E R . E E L . O W L
```

48

```
L A I C . A S C A P . O T T O
E B R O . M I L L E . F O R M
A L A N . A L I C E . C L U E
H E S F A R T O O W O O D E N
. . E Y E . A I N U .
U M B R E L L A . T E R E S A
N Y E . L A I D . A S T E R
H E S A T E R R I B L E H A M
I L O V E . K E R R . A L E
D O M I N I . D E E P E N E D
. A T M O . A A R .
H E D R O P S H I S L I N E S
A G R I . A T E S T . V I V A
V A N E . L I S L E . A C E S
E N O S . E A S E D . N E N E
```

49

```
R I F T . . . T O L L . Q U A D
I O L A . . R O S I E . I S L E
P U A D R U Q E D S . C E D E .
E S T . O N U S . S U T R A S .
. . P A G E . M E N U . . . . .
T O U R S . S O N O R A N T . .
H O V I S . R I T E . E L I A .
E R I C . D A Z E D . S T E M .
S I N K . E V E S . A P A C E .
A C E T A T E S . I N U R E . .
. E T O N . E R N E . . . . . .
S T A M E N . F R A U . O D E .
C I N Q . A P U A Q L A N E D .
A R T E . T O R S I . F L A G .
B E E R . E R L E . T Y N E . .
```

50

```
D A Y C A R E . H A P . F I R
E R E C T O R . O T H E L L O
W E L C O M E . G O A L I E S
. A P P L E . M G M S L T D S
. S L O P E . S E E . . . . .
P I N K . E T C . N I G H . .
E M I G R E S . U A R . S A Y
T A X B A S E . D R U M S U P
A G O . P E T . G A G R U L E
L E N A . A B E . T E S S . .
. S A O . B L I S S . . . . .
L B J S B V D S . D I V E R .
A M O E B A E . E L E C T O R
C O N S O L E . D E G R A D E
E C G . T S P . T R E S S E D
```

51

```
A U N T . S H E . S P R I T
D R E S S . M E X . T E A C H
A G L E T . U M P . U T T E R
M E L T I N G P O T . E I R E
. S L O G . S U C R O S E . .
M A K E T T L E . G A P . . .
U S A . S E E L . R A Z O R .
L I N D . D R I F T . N E M O
E A T U P . O R A S . T I P .
. S E C . T E M P L A T E . .
P R E T Z E L . E P E E . . .
H E R B . O U T L A N D I S H
A A R O N . Z O O . C O N T E
S T O W E . O N A . E F F I E
E A R L Y . N E D . F O R D .
```

52

```
B A T S . F E E L S . L O B .
A C R E . A X L E S . E A S E
C H I E F T A I N S C R Y A T
H E M . E C C E . O M E G A .
. B R A T . B E N A R E S . .
A R R A N T . F A N G S . . .
H O E R . P I N T O . A D S .
A B A B Y L O N C O U N C I L
B E D . O A S E S . A M M O .
. E N T E R . L A M E S T . .
M E A N D E R . F A T E . . .
E L I D E . L O C O . A D E .
S U M E R I S I C U M E N I N
S T A R . R O M A N . T E R I
Y E T . S T E L A . A W E D .
```

53

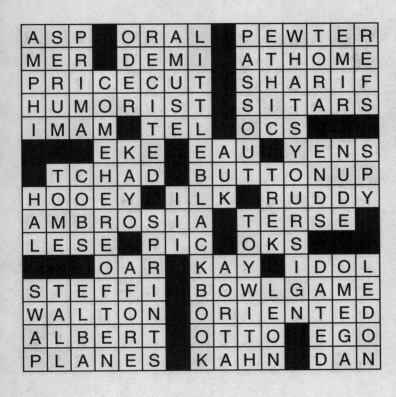

```
A S P   O R A L   P E W T E R
M E R   D E M I   A T H O M E
P R I C E C U T   S H A R I F
H U M O R I S T   S I T A R S
I M A M   T E L   O C S
  E K E   E A U   Y E N S
  T C H A D   B U T T O N U P
H O O E Y   I L K   R U D D Y
A M B R O S I A   T E R S E
L E S E   P I C   O K S
  O A R   K A Y   I D O L
S T E F F I   B O W L G A M E
W A L T O N   O R I E N T E D
A L B E R T   O T T O   E G O
P L A N E S   K A H N   D A N
```

54

```
T H E E     C A L M   M A T
S A G A N   S Y R U P   I R A
P H O T O F I N I S H   D I N
    P U R I S T   N D A K
  C H E A T   C E R E A L
C H E E R U P   E L D E R S
H E A R   R A V E   M A M I E
I R R   H E R A L D S   A V E
T U T T I   K N E E   P R A M
A B O A R D   V E H I C L E
  F R E E A S   P A T H S
L O G S   P R A Y E R
A G O   C E N T E R S T A G E
I L L   U N I O N   H O M E R
T E D   E D E N     M A T E
```

55

```
M I M E   W H A R F   A W O L
I L A Y   H A N T A   R O M E
N I N E L E T T E R S L O N G
T E N D E R I S   T H E S I S
    S E N   S H U N
A D O P T S   W H I T   T O M
S E P I A   K H A N   G E N E
W R I T T E N I N G E R M A N
A R N A   M E T E   R A P I D
N Y E   A B L E   S O B E R S
    O M I T   P E T
T W O B I T   M E D I A T E S
S E V E N T E E N A C R O S S
A R E S   E N A C T   C O S T
R E N E   R E L E E   O N E S
```

56

```
D E A L S   S D A K   A A A A
O R B I T   H E R O   W W I I
J O L L Y R A J A H   F O R M
O S E   G I L A   O V U L E S
    H I N T   D U A L
M A J O A D   B A T T L E O F
A T O W N   A R N E   Y A L E
M A I D   F L A S K   S T E N
E L S A   O I N K   P A N I C
T E T H E R E D   T H R O N E
    Y A W N   H A R I
A U R O R A   S E R E   E G E
B R A U   R A N E E N O S E S
B A N D   D R O P   I D I O T
A L S O   S E W S   A D A L E
```

57

```
C O D S   S L A V   J E H A D
O P E C   H O W E   O N E M O
M A J A   T O O L   S A R E E
B L A C K E N L A S T B O X
    C I T Y   Z E L L
M I C H E L   S Q U E E Z E D
A T A I L   G A U S S   L A O
N A R C   A R L E S   B O S N
O L E   K L U T Z   M E T E D
F O R G R A B S   L A D Y D I
    I A M S   C I N Q
T U R N T O T H E S O U T H H
I R A N I   A U N T   I R A E
C A N I O   K I T E   L A I R
O L D E N   E T O N   T Y R E
```

58

```
    A L A M B   A R C E D
    A R E Y O U   D E I D R E
S T A G E D R A M E T H Y S T
W A B E   E L L I S   C S A
A L I S T   E T T E   O L E S
T E A   R O T O   T R E N T
    T A F T S   M E N A C E
P E A R L F A T H A H I N E S
A R M I E S   R A K E S
W R O T E   A T E E   W A G
P A R E   S E T S   S M I L E
A T A   H A U T E   E L A N
W I L L I A M S A P P H I R E
    C L A R K E   N E A T L Y
    Y E S E S   D E L A Y
```

59

```
S W A T S   L A Z E   I T S Y
L A R R Y   A D E N   I R A E
I I I I M N M Z N G   I O T A
P T A   B A B E   R E N D E R
    I O N S   C A N T
S H E I L A   P A V E M E N T
T A X I S   D A M E   A C A R
A S T I   S O W E D   T O T E
B O R N   C L E O   B O L T S
S N A T C H E D   H O N E Y S
    A P E S   C O O S
B O T T O M   L O U S   S P A
O L E O   I I I R R T A T O N
P L A N   N O O K   E M E N D
S A M S   G U N S   D A N D Y
```

60

```
H A S A T   S T I F F   H A T
E L L I E   T O M E I   O N O
F O U N T A I N P E N   K I T
T E E T H I N G   A D E L E
    E R G   D E L A Y E D
B O W E R Y   L E T S U P
O L I N S   M O A T   N O L A
L I N T   E A G L E   T K O S
D O E R   R I O T   L E E D S
    C A V I L S   L A D Y I N
P H O N I C S   K E W
L O O T S   I N A S E N S E
E L L   A L U M I N U M C A N
A L E   G A Z E S   I M A G O
S Y R   E D I T H   T Y R E S
```

61

62

63

64

65

R	O	A	D	S	■	G	L	O	W	■	S	C	A	R
C	O	L	I	C	■	L	A	V	A	■	H	O	M	E
A	MPH	I	T	H	E	A	T	E	R	■	E	M	I	L
■	■	T	I	N	D	E	R	■	A	MPH	O	R	A	■
■	B	O	O	S	T	E	R	■	F	L	O	S	S	Y
P	O	T	■	M	R	S	■	P	L	O	W	■	■	■
E	L	A	P	S	E	■	A	R	A	P	A	H	O	■
A	U	R	A	■	A	B	E	■	■	R	A	G	A	■
■	S	Y	MPH	O	N	I	C	■	M	A	D	R	I	D
■	L	A	U	D	■	T	A	M	■	E	V	A	■	■
D	E	S	E	R	T	■	M	A	T	I	S	S	E	■
W	E	L	T	S	■	H	E	R	E	A	T	■	■	■
E	R	I	E	■	C	A	MPH	O	R	B	A	L	L	S
L	I	M	E	■	A	L	I	T	■	L	E	A	V	E
L	E	E	R	■	B	E	S	S	■	E	L	G	I	N

66

S	I	M	B	A	■	M	A	R	C	■	E	B	O	N
T	R	A	L	A	■	E	R	O	O	■	J	U	N	E
R	A	Z	O	R	C	L	A	M	S	■	E	C	C	E
A	T	E	S	■	L	I	P	S	M	A	C	K	E	R
P	E	R	S	I	A	N	■	■	O	R	T	S	■	■
■	■	O	N	S	A	L	E	■	■	P	E	K	E	S
A	R	O	M	A	S	■	E	M	U	■	D	I	V	A
R	A	N	■	S	E	L	F	I	S	H	■	N	I	M
I	T	E	M	■	S	E	T	■	H	A	S	S	L	E
D	E	L	O	S	■	A	S	S	E	N	T	■	■	■
■	■	I	R	O	N	■	O	R	G	A	N	I	C	■
S	I	N	G	L	E	F	I	L	E	■	N	O	N	A
I	D	E	A	■	S	A	N	D	D	O	L	L	A	R
T	O	R	N	■	T	I	R	E	■	L	E	A	N	T
E	L	S	A	■	S	T	I	R	■	D	Y	N	E	S

67

S	W	I	G	■	F	E	E	S	■	W	A	I	L	■
L	E	N	A	■	L	A	L	A	■	P	E	A	S	E
A	A	R	D	V	A	R	K	S	■	E	N	A	T	E
B	R	I	G	I	T	■	S	H	O	P	T	A	L	K
■	■	E	A	T	S	■	A	R	S	I	N	E	S	■
B	E	A	T	N	I	K	S	■	B	I	N	D	■	■
R	C	A	■	D	R	I	P	S	■	S	T	A	T	S
I	R	A	S	■	E	N	A	C	T	■	O	A	H	U
C	U	B	I	C	■	S	T	O	O	L	■	R	E	N
■	■	A	N	A	T	■	S	O	R	E	S	P	O	T
E	S	T	A	D	O	S	■	T	A	M	E	■	■	■
B	A	T	T	E	N	E	D	■	T	O	N	I	T	E
O	V	E	R	T	■	A	A	R	O	N	S	R	O	D
N	O	R	A	S	■	T	I	E	R	■	E	A	T	A
D	R	Y	S	■	O	S	S	A	■	D	E	E	M	■

68

R	A	Z	E	■	C	L	O	Y	■	G	L	I	N	T
O	R	E	L	■	R	A	V	E	■	R	I	N	S	E
Y	A	N	K	E	E	S	I	S	E	E	K	N	A	Y
■	■	■	S	P	E	D	■	R	A	E	■	■	■	■
S	C	O	O	T	E	R	■	E	N	S	N	A	R	L
A	R	I	S	E	S	■	C	L	A	Y	■	R	O	E
R	I	L	K	E	■	S	H	I	N	■	S	T	O	W
■	M	I	A	M	I	T	O	T	I	M	A	I	M	■
P	E	E	R	■	N	O	M	E	■	E	L	S	I	E
O	A	S	■	S	T	O	P	■	G	R	A	T	E	S
I	N	T	O	N	E	D	■	S	L	I	D	E	R	S
■	■	■	F	O	R	■	J	E	A	N	■	■	■	■
B	O	S	T	O	N	D	I	D	N	O	T	S	O	B
U	P	S	E	T	■	A	V	E	C	■	R	O	B	E
T	E	E	N	Y	■	M	E	R	E	■	E	X	I	T

69

```
T E R P   V E G A S   D I S T
E X E S   E L E N I   E W E R
A P I A   S I N G L E F I L E
  O N L Y T H E L O N E L Y
  M I S U S E   D A L E
H O U S E       T O T
A Y N   L E D G E R   S A K E
N E T   D R E A M O N   G I L
A Z O V   R E P U T E   R E B
  A B S       G U A V A
  A B L E   S U E D E S
  S O L E S U R V I V O R S
L O N E R A N G E R   P I T A
I N D Y   I N E R T   E G E R
B E S S   L I S T S   N A M E
```

70

```
S H A F T   S L O G   O K R A
T E R R E   H I L O   A N E T
E N R O L   I N A T   S O S O
I C A N L I F E F O R T W O
N E S T O R S   P I S A N S
  D N A   M O O G   B A H
G A P E   M O N T H S O N A
A N A S S   E V A   T O U C H
M A R K T W A I N   U T E S
U L A   R A T E   I S T
T O M C A T   I S T H M U S
  G O O D C O M P L I M E N T
P I U S   H O A R   L O N G A
G E N T   E Z R A   E S S E N
A S T A   S E X Y   S T A R K
```

71

```
H O O F   S E M I S   C L A P
E D G E   T R A C T   H E R O
M O L E B O O T C A P I T O L
P R E T E N S E   C E R I S E
    G E E   S C E P T E R
M E T H O D   C H A P
O C E A N   S L O T   I R A S
B U N K E R H A R O L D A N T
S A T E   E A S T   A O R T A
    L A M P   S P L E E N
C A R V E R S   S I D
E L A I N E   M O N O C L E S
S A M S A N J U A N G R A N T
A M B I   D E L V E   I N G E
R O O T   S T E E R   B E R M
```

72

```
O M E G A   D A L E   O P T S
R E L I C   E D A M   L O R E
A L E R T   I D L E   E D E N
D E M & I N G   O R G & I E S
  O V E N S   G R E A S E
S T O L E S   C H E E R
L O G E   T A R O   A S S E T
E R R   A S S A U L T   & R E
D E E M S   S P R Y   F E T A
  A S O N E   S T A R E S
S C A L A R   S H E E R
A L M & I N E   I S L & E R S
G I B E   A V I D   F O L I O
A M I R   T I L E   E L I O T
N E T S   E L K S   R E S T S
```

73

```
CHIC . KASEM . SLY .
AUTO . OSTIA . LYON .
BRONXTHANX . ENDO
. TATER . IBEXES
TIMEXES . APPLE
ERASER . PARISH
PANTS . MURAL . ASK
INXS . EATEN . GLUE
DIP . INDIA . TRAIN
. HIDDEN . BEENTO
INANE . RELAXES
MEREST . CARET .
AMYS . SPHINXJINX
MENS . AIOLI . OKAY
. AXE . REUSE . BENZ
```

74

```
JAILS . PAP . EWER
ULNAE . IHAD . MARE
DOQMENTARYFILMS
DOB . FAT . SNORTAT
SPIRIT . BEER
. ATALL . SMEARS
AMAN . NOOP . ALLIE
POCKETCALQLATOR
PREEN . ITER . PITA
TORRID . EXECS .
. GOAD . AREOLA
ASSUMES . FLU . CIS
QLINARYDELIGHTS
RUDI . SOON . SAREE
AMEX . UND . EGEST
```

75

```
ASCAP . SAKI . POEM
STELA . AVIS . IPSO
COSEC . LECH . GEST
HATCHBACK . AGREE
. SIAM . ABEYANT
ONE . SCI . PROB .
GOTHIC . COINAGES
LUAU . ADIOS . CATO
ENSNARED . BIKINI
. CRAN . SAR . TAR
ESTHETE . KNOT
SLOBS . GREENBACK
TARA . FAIL . MOREL
OTIC . ITAL . ANILE
PECK . RELY . NEALE
```

76

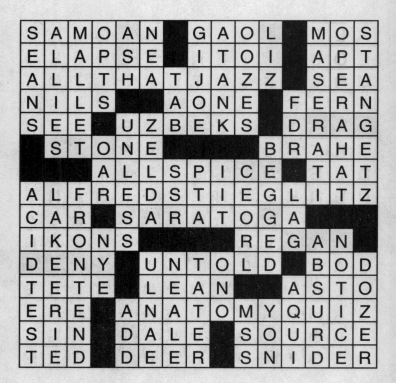

```
SAMOAN . GAOL . MOS
ELAPSE . ITOI . APT
ALLTHATJAZZ . SEA
NILS . AONE . FERN
SEE . UZBEKS . DRAG
. STONE . BRAHE
. ALLSPICE . TAT
ALFREDSTIEGLITZ
CAR . SARATOGA .
IKONS . REGAN
DENY . UNTOLD . BOD
TETE . LEAN . ASTO
ERE . ANATOMYQUIZ
SIN . DALE . SOURCE
TED . DEER . SNIDER
```

77

H	A	D	J	■	S	C	A	R	■	Z	A	P	P	A
E	L	I	A	■	W	A	L	E	■	E	R	R	O	L
A	L	E	C	■	A	N	O	N	■	A	G	O	R	A
D	O	N	K	E	Y	O	T	E	■	L	O	W	E	R
■	■	■	S	M	E	E	■	■	B	O	N	■	■	■
P	A	S	T	E	D	■	F	L	A	T	■	P	A	R
I	N	U	R	E	■	L	A	I	R	■	T	A	L	E
E	D	G	A	R	R	I	C	E	B	U	R	R	O	S
C	R	A	W	■	A	M	E	N	■	S	U	S	H	I
E	E	R	■	R	I	O	T	■	D	E	M	E	A	N
■	■	■	Z	E	N	■	■	H	A	R	P	■	■	■
B	E	B	O	P	■	M	C	A	S	S	C	H	E	R
A	D	O	R	E	■	R	A	S	H	■	A	U	R	A
B	E	R	R	A	■	E	S	T	E	■	R	E	I	N
E	R	G	O	T	■	D	E	E	R	■	D	Y	E	D

78

A	C	H	E	■	C	H	A	N	■	■	A	B	L	E
R	A	I	N	■	H	E	L	E	N	■	G	L	O	W
A	N	N	E	■	E	D	D	I	E	■	E	A	S	E
B	E	D	■	L	E	G	A	L	T	E	N	D	E	R
■	■	■	R	A	I	S	E	■	W	A	D	E	R	S
G	R	A	N	D	E	■	F	L	O	R	A	■	■	■
R	E	N	T	S	■	P	E	A	R	L	■	H	A	N
O	N	C	E	■	T	R	A	C	K	■	L	U	R	E
W	O	E	■	P	R	O	S	E	■	H	A	S	T	E
■	■	■	F	O	I	S	T	■	T	E	T	H	E	R
C	A	S	A	L	S	■	■	H	A	R	E	M	■	■
R	A	T	T	L	E	S	N	A	K	E	■	O	R	E
A	R	I	A	■	C	L	O	V	E	■	A	N	E	W
T	O	L	L	■	T	A	P	E	R	■	G	E	N	E
E	N	T	E	■	■	P	E	N	S	■	E	Y	E	S

79

F	L	E	E	■	S	C	A	T	S	■	C	A	M	E
L	O	L	L	■	P	E	N	A	L	■	I	R	O	N
E	R	I	E	■	E	N	T	R	E	■	G	E	N	E
W	I	S	C	O	N	S	I	N	D	I	A	N	A	■
■	■	■	T	I	D	E	S	■	■	G	R	A	D	■
T	A	N	■	L	A	D	■	P	A	L	■	■	■	■
A	L	E	A	■	■	A	L	L	O	T	T	E	D	■
N	E	W	M	E	X	I	C	O	L	O	R	A	D	O
A	C	T	I	V	I	S	T	■	■	A	M	E	N	■
■	■	■	I	V	A	■	P	T	A	■	E	N	G	■
■	B	A	S	T	■	A	L	I	N	E	■	■	■	■
■	O	K	L	A	H	O	M	A	R	Y	L	A	N	D
S	O	R	E	■	I	L	O	N	A	■	A	L	E	E
A	L	O	P	■	G	L	U	E	D	■	N	A	I	L
C	A	N	T	■	H	A	R	T	E	■	D	I	L	L

80

B	Y	T	E	■	R	A	M	A	R	■	A	B	O	U
O	O	H	S	■	A	L	I	C	E	■	D	A	B	S
I	K	E	S	■	T	I	D	E	S	■	E	C	O	N
L	E	W	■	T	I	E	D	■	I	M	A	K	E	A
■	■	■	E	U	R	O	■	L	A	Z	U	L	I	■
B	A	S	S	E	S	■	E	D	I	T	■	N	I	P
A	N	T	S	Y	■	P	O	I	N	T	■	T	S	E
T	I	E	R	■	B	E	F	O	G	■	O	H	N	O
I	S	R	■	D	A	R	T	S	■	C	R	E	O	N
K	E	N	■	A	R	C	H	■	Q	U	E	S	T	S
■	■	■	F	I	T	T	H	E	■	U	R	S	A	■
M	A	R	L	E	E	■	R	I	O	T	■	D	B	A
B	O	O	K	■	R	O	O	S	T	■	A	D	E	N
A	N	N	A	■	■	E	R	A	S	E	■	O	L	E	O
S	E	T	S	■	D	O	D	O	S	■	K	E	R	N

81

```
MARS   SOSAD  FARO
OREL   ALIVE  AMOK
ERLE   GALEN  LALA
SEEEE EVENTUALLY
 SAKE  SUET   FEE
ITS  KATIE  THIRD
REEF  PIA  PEA
ADDRESS  TORNADO
   ADE  MIR  KNEW
SLING  COCKY  ASE
IAM  ETON  ESCE
SUPPRESSSSSTORY
TRUE  NITTI  ENTO
EIRE  ONEAL  EDEL
REEK  FERRO  LARK
```

82

```
UTA   GOTHAM  HAD
BELT  IDOIDO  ICE
OSCILLOGRAM  SHE
LLANO  STREETER
TANGRAM  ENTO
  LENORE  TOGAS
RISE  ONOR  UNRIP
ELO  ANAGRAM  ANA
ASCOT  DUAL  EMTS
PAINT  SENDIN
  ODES  TANGLED
MAGENTAS  SAONE
OUR  DACTYLOGRAM
BRA  TIRADE  ECTO
YAM  ORENSE  AES
```

83

```
  PRIGS  ISIAH
CHIVALRY  INTONE
AUSTRIAN  MEANIE
MLA  EGS  RIP  LLD
ELIJAHS  ENTRY
 DUST  PCT  ILED
SPAT  URIAH  DIVA
TOM  PHONE  VAL
ALOW  MONTA  MENE
ROUE  YDS  RUNT
 TESLA  EMPOWER
EPH  HIS  LYE  INO
LIFEOF  CONNECTS
ACUATE  AGODDESS
SALTS  NEWSY
```

84

```
LOCO  FLOSS  SHAQ
INON  REBUT  LULU
ZEUS  ANISE  UNIE
 NEBUTTHEBRAVE
PASTEL  ILL  NEG
ODE  NEAT  YIP
LOLA  ILIE  PAISA
ABOMINABLESWMAN
RERAN  IBEX  SPUN
 NCO  SECO  RTE
ARK  AHA  ENSUES
MANISANISLAND
ACES  RENAL  AERO
ZEAL  ANGLE  KNOW
ERDA  STEED  ETON
```

```
S A V E ■ B A I L S ■ P I T A
E M I L ■ U N I O N ■ R N A S
C O N C E R T I N O ■ E T U I
T R E A C L E ■ G U S S E T S
■ ■ J O Y ■ B E T T E R ■ ■
E T O N ■ O A R ■ A L M A S
G M A N ■ A R K ■ A L L E G E
A C R ■ P R E L U D E ■ Z E E
R E A S O N ■ A S S ■ E Z R A
D E N T I ■ A V E ■ E N O S ■
■ ■ T E R E S A ■ P I L ■ ■
O M E L E T S ■ M A N I A C S
B I L L ■ H U M O R E S Q U E
E L L A ■ I R A T E ■ T U R N
Y E A R ■ C E N S E ■ S A L T
```

```
H O P E S ■ N B C ■ W I M P
O P I N E ■ C U Y P ■ A R A L
L E E I A C O C C A ■ G A L A
I N C A S H ■ L E G E N D S
E L E C ■ E N D E A R ■ G E T
S Y S ■ C R E E ■ N O N A M E
■ ■ M A Y N T ■ W A T E R ■
E D G A R L E E M A S T E R S
■ N U R S E ■ S O L O S ■ ■
G R A S S Y ■ T R O N ■ C S T
R A Y ■ T O A S T S ■ S O T O
A C A J O U S ■ E S C O R T
V E R A ■ R O B E R T E L E E
E L E M ■ E N I D ■ O N E A M
S L A B ■ E O S ■ P E R K S
```

```
B A G S ■ S C A L P ■ O P T S
E L I A ■ C A B E R ■ M A I L
D E L I B E R A T E H A S T E
S E A L A N E ■ A N T A E ■
■ ■ L I T T L E G I A N T
T O L T E C ■ A I D E S ■ ■
A M E E R ■ T R A I N ■ E T E
M E N D ■ M A H R E ■ F R I T
E N D ■ D O M E S ■ D I A N A
■ A E R I E ■ P O R T A L ■
L E A D B A L L O O N ■ ■
U L T R A ■ G L U T T E D
N E W E R T R A D I T I O N S
E V A N ■ R E B E C ■ D O O M
S E R O ■ E B O N Y ■ E L L S
```

```
A K I M ■ A P E S ■ S T O A
A M I N O ■ M E N U ■ T W I G
M A T T B I O N D I ■ A Y L A
A L T O H O R N ■ T A B L E T
■ ■ L I T E ■ B A L L A D E
F A J I T A ■ S U B L E T ■
E A R N S ■ G U I L E ■ H A D
D A R E ■ A I S L E ■ H A Z E
S S T ■ S P L I T ■ F O R U M
O R I O L E ■ A L L P R O ■
S I L E N T S ■ A L A E ■ ■
R A K I S H ■ D I E T S O D A
T M E N ■ E L D O C T O R O W
A B I E ■ G O A L ■ O N C U E
S I N D ■ M A Y I ■ P E A R
```

89

```
T K O S . S P E E D . B A N E
I N R E . O U T T O . U B E R
N O R A . I S A A C S T E R N
T W I L I G H T . T A T T O O
. N I N N Y . G O N E . . .
A T H O M E . H A R D S H I P
C R A N E . S A V O Y . O L E
C O T S . B E D E W . T W I T
R O C . B A G E L . Q U A K E
A P H E L I O N . P U R R E R
. . . R A T S . G R A N D .
C L E A R S . B A E D E K E R
J E S S E H E L M S . D E L E
A N T E . O N E A T . T E E N
M O O R . P A B L O . O L E O
```

90

```
B A R B . C H A K A . T A K E
O R A L . R A T E L . O M E N
O C T O . E Y E P O P P I N G
T H E C A T I N T H E [HAT]
H I D . Y E N . A N S E L M
S E R G E . G O P . . L I I
. W A R . N E C K T I E S
M O N E Y T [HAT] S W [HAT] I W A N T
E V A N E S C E . S O I
G E R . . H T S . S N O R E
A R C A R O . T E K . R E G
. W I L L I A M S [HAT] N E R
S W I N G M U S I C . P A V E
K A L E . O P I N E . I T E S
A X E D . S E N S E . N E S S
```

91

```
J A K E . C E S A R . A H A B
E X I T . A S K M E . M O V E
A L D A . S T E A L . O P E C
N E W . S T A W H I L E I C K
. I C H O R . M O B . .
A R T H U R . P E N T A G O N
C O H A N . S A V E S . T I O
T O D D . K E Y E D . D O L T
O N E . H A L E S . B E G E T
R E D O U B L E . T O L E D O
. N M I . C R U E T .
B E T H E B U S H A T . H A J
R A M A . B R E A D . M E N U
I S A N . L E A S E . I R O N
M E N D . E A T E R . B O N O
```

92

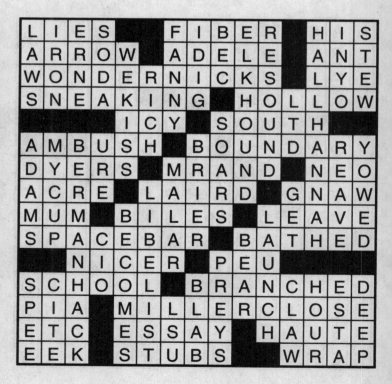

```
L I E S . F I B E R . H I S
A R R O W . A D E L E . A N T
W O N D E R N I C K S . L Y E
S N E A K I N G . H O L L O W
. . I C Y . S O U T H .
A M B U S H . B O U N D A R Y
D Y E R S . M R A N D . N E O
A C R E . L A I R D . G N A W
M U M . B I L E S . L E A V E
S P A C E B A R . B A T H E D
. N I C E R . P E U .
S C H O O L . B R A N C H E D
P I A . M I L L E R C L O S E
E T C . E S S A Y . H A U T E
E E K . S T U B S . W R A P
```

93

```
R I F L E   E M E N D   L A G
E R R O R   D I V E R   A R E
M A O R I   I N A F A M I L Y
  M I N U T E   T I N E S
D E B S   S E R A C   D E N E
A V A   P E D A L E D   S E R
D I C T A   L A D E S
A L K A L I S   R E F A C E D
  R E N T A   E N U R E
A R C   S T A R T E R   T O N
C E R E   O R R I S   A S S T
A M E N S   A N K L E T
C O M E A L O N G   I T W A S
I T E   L A N G E   S N O R T
A E S   E P E E S   T A S S E
```

94

```
C A P A   B A S H   C L A E S
U S E S   O G L E   H I N G E
R E A P   N E A R   O L D I E
B A S I L M E T A B O L I S M
S T E R E O       A C E
      E T T U   A S H   B A S
H O A R   L A S S O   O R T
A N I S E T H E S I O L O G Y
Z E D   L E A S E   O N Y X
E S E   E S Q   S L A V
    S M L   I C E C A P
E X S P E A R M I N T A L L Y
A R K I N   I A T E   B E A R
S A I N T   B L E U   L A N E
T Y P E S   S I M P   E N D S
```

95

```
E A S E S   I N F E R   M I T
C R E T E   M E A R A   O R R
O M A H A   P E A A Y E T E E
  Y A L T A     S T O N E
E T O N   A L T O S   A R E S
L O U   S T E A M E R
M O T E T   C A R E S S E R
E L E G I E S   R E L I E V E
R E A G E N T S   A R E A S
    B E E O H E X   A N E
R E M O   S P O O K   E R S T
A L A R M   M E T R E
J A Y E Y E G E E   R A W L S
A T E   T R I E R   I T H O T
H E R   H E L L S   G O Y A S
```

96

```
R E N E W   B A A L   A M O S
I C A M E   E R L E   B O L E
S C R U B   E M I L   E T A L
K E Y   B O R S K A R L O F F
    H E R   E N E
E D E A D A M S   D E F A M E
D A R N   L E T T   L O M A N
D I O S   E E R I E   R I N D
I S S E L   K I E L   E S T O
E Y E L I D   A R T E S H A W
      P E S   O N T
C R A G S T E V E N S   L E S
L O G E   E V A N   I N E R T
A L A N   S E N D   G E N I I
M E R E   T R E S   N A D E R
```

237

```
A L T O   M I A M I   A G O G
M O R N   A C T O N   R O B E
E R A T O O H A N I G L O O
N I C H E   M O T   N U D E S
S S T E X C E S S   D E M
    L O U       S I D E R S
A B B A   R A G T A G   D I A
L L A M A F R E E F O R A L L
P U G   P E E D E E   E L E E
S E A C O W       L A D
    T U G   D D A Y R A N D D
S W E D E   R I B   F L O U R
E E L D E V O T E E   E L M O
R I L L   I N K E R   R I P S
F L E E   M E A T Y   T E S S
```

```
A B L E   C H E W   S E A M
L E O S   H O M E   H A N O I
F L A T   E V I L   O R G A N
A T D A Y S E N D   F L I T S
        I S L E   H A Y E S
  F A C E   S N E E R S
C A M E L S   T A M   T A L L
A M E N D E D   R E G A L I A
T E N T   T A R   N U R S E D
    E L U D E S   E T O N
  S C R A P   T A P S
L O A F S   M I D S T R E A M
A F R O S   A N D A   A L M A
S A L L E   P U L L   S L O T
  R O D S   S E E M   H A S H
```

```
P S I   A U L D   A L A M O
A C H   S H E A   D R A P E D
P E A C H F E Z   E D W I N S
E N V O I   S E A M U S
R E E L E D   T O O   A M S
      S T E A M T U R B A N
S S S   T H A R   E S T A T E
U C L A   T N T   E S T A
S O A R E D   I O N S   E E K
H U C K L E B E R E T
I R K   E S E   W I N T E R
    O M E G A S   P E A L E
S H I V E R   G I V E A T A M
R E G E N T   E D E N   U N U
S N O R T   R E E D   M D S
```

```
A S P E R A   C U T E S T
L E A P E D   H A R R O W E D
L A M O D E   E N G I N E E R
    P U L S A T E S   E T I
G A M E B A L L     T H E
H A Y E S   E T H   J A P E S
Q U M   H E H A D A S O R T
  O F C O P Y R I G H T
O N T H E B I B L E   A D O
B E H A N   N R A   M A T E D
T R E   E N V I R O N S
A I R   N A G A S A K I
I N T H E P O T   P A S S U P
N E H E M I A H   I D E A T E
  S E C O N D   D O N N E R
```

```
G A R B A G E   E M P I R I C
E C U A D O R   G R E N A D A
T H E R E I S N O S A D D E R
S E R B   N E O   R O S E S
    S E T   R B I S
F A B   B O O M E R   S G T S
O V I N E   M A R K T W A I N
S O L A R I A   I S R A E L I
S I G H T T H A N   I N L E T
E R E S   T A R G E T   S R S
    C O S T   R E D
B E L L E   I R A   A R I A
A Y O U N G P E S S I M I S T
R E A C T O R   V E D E T T E
E R N E S T O   P R E S T O N
```

```
A L O H A   A S P S   S A L E
L I B E L   S C O T   T I E D
A (THE) I S M   S (OLD) E R   A R (MAN) I
    S O S   S T E R N E S T
A C C E N T S   S E E D
P O L   D O U R   P R I N T S
P A I R   U S E S   A N E R A
E R N E S T H E M I N G W A Y
A S I D E   I V A N   S A D E
R E C E N T   E R D A   G E R
    E N I D   T I L L E R S
E G O M A N I A   A P E
C (AND) L E   G A (THE) R   H O T (SEA) T
R E A R   E N N A   A N O L E
U R N S   D A S H   S E N S E
```

```
D E W   B E L A B O R   T A D
A Y E   E X A M I N E   H M O
G E T O N E S I D E A   G A S
    R I C H   S O L T I   I
B E F O G       M I R E
E L O   N A G A N O   E G A D
L A R D   D O T E D   I N R I
O N T O   D R O N E   N I M S
I T H E   T E N E T   G M A N
T R E S   O D E S S A   O R E
    A C T S       T A C K Y
    O O Z E S   H A H A
J E U   E R U T U F E H T O T
I A N   L I N E M A N   A X E
M R T   L E S T E R S   N Y X
```

```
C A L F   S T A I R   A B I E
O L E O   P A N N E   P A D S
B E A U T I C I A N   I R O N
B E N N E T T   E N A B L E
    T R E   B E G O N E
H E M A N   M A Y A N   R I B
A L A I   S E C E D E   S R O
L I N N E T S   F E T C H E D
L O I   N E S S U S   A O N E
E T C   A R E E L   L U P E S
    U T T E R S   O A T
C O R R E O   E L L I P S E
A M I E   S H A M P O O I N G
R O S E   E R N I E   U N I O
P O T S   T H A T S   S A P S
```

105

```
FEAT  ROBOT  TURN
AMUR  EDITH  OLEO
DUNE  FATHERLAND
ESTATES  ORIENTE
     ITER    MAR
CAESARS  ISLAMIC
ELM  LATER  STOOL
ADAM  LYRES  ETTA
REMAN  LANAI  HAW
ARENOSE  ENDLESS
    AIT    DEAR
FIACRES  MUSCLES
UNCLEREMUS  TOLA
ERTE  RUARK  IDOL
LOAD  OLNEY  CENT
```

106

```
LEASH  ROOF  SAMS
ALLIE  EARL  AGEE
WADDLEITBE  FILE
SMA  PANS  SHARED
    MESS  CHARLES
COMEDY  MAORI
UVEA  SINUS  OWE
BELLYUPTOTHEBAA
ART  ALLEN  VOLT
   ALTAR  CREEKS
HARRIET  LAIR
USURER  AERO  SHA
RISE  ITSMYTWEET
ODES  OHIO  ERASE
NEST  RYAN  DYLAN
```